Lessons for Living

Reflections on
the Weekly Bible Readings
and on the Festivals

Sidney Greenberg

Foreword by **Harold S. Kushner**

HARTMORE HOUSE
New York & Bridgeport

LIBRARY OF CONGRESS CATALOGING-IN-PUBLICATION DATA

Greenberg, Sidney, 1917–
    Lessons for living.

    1. Bible. O.T. Pentateuch—Sermons.   2. Festival-day
sermons, Jewish.   3. Jewish sermons—United States.
4. Sermons, American—Jewish authors.   I. Title.
BS1225.4.G74   1985   296.4′2   85-14024
ISBN 0-87677-157-6

For
Elisha and Daniella
Ilana and Darone

with love and hope

BOOKS BY RABBI SIDNEY GREENBERG

Inspirational Essays:

Adding Life to Our Years
Finding Ourselves
Hidden Hungers
Say Yes to Life

Anthologies:

A Treasury of Comfort
The Bar Mitzvah Companion (Co-Editor)
A Modern Treasury of Jewish Thoughts
A Treasury of the Art of Living
Teaching and Preaching: High Holiday Bible Themes
    Volume 1: Rosh Hashanah
    Volume 2: Yom Kippur

Youth Prayer Books:

Siddurenu (Co-Editor)
High Holiday Services for Children
Sabbath and Festival Services for Children
A Contemporary High Holiday Service (Co-Editor)
The New Model Seder (Co-Editor)
Junior Contemporary Prayer Book for the High Holidays (Co-Editor)

Prayer Books:

Contemporary Prayers and Readings
    for the High Holidays, Sabbaths, and Special Occasions
Likrat Shabbat: Worship, Study, and Song
    for Sabbath and Festival Evenings (Co-Editor)
The New Maḥzor for Rosh Hashanah and Yom Kippur (Co-Editor)

Contents

EXODUS

LEVITICUS

NUMBERS

DEUTERONOMY

HOLY DAYS, FESTIVALS, AND SPECIAL OCCASIONS

Foreword

THE PUBLICATION of this book corrects a long-standing injustice. Why should the congregants of Temple Sinai in suburban Philadelphia be the sole beneficiaries of Rabbi Sidney Greenberg's wit and wisdom? Why should his weekly insights reach only the readers of Philadelphia's *Jewish Exponent*, while those of us who live elsewhere are deprived of them? It is simply not fair. And while there are many instances of life's unfairness which are beyond our power to correct, I am pleased that this one has been set right with the appearance of *Lessons for Living*.

The virtues of Rabbi Greenberg's preaching and writing will become clear to the reader from the opening pages of this book. First, he has an unerring eye for truths which are both profound and simple. His messages are not only clever, they are important. He says things which we need to hear, things we should have figured out for ourselves but somehow never did. (It has been said that one way to recognize a great truth is by our reaction of "of course, why didn't I think of that myself?")

While some writers glory in their ability to baffle the ordinary reader, to appear profound when in truth they are only obscure, Rabbi Greenberg delights in being understandable. Indeed, he is known (as rabbi and writer) for being accessible! His messages are for everyone, Jew and gentile, scholar and neophyte, wise or otherwise.

Another characteristic of Sidney Greenberg's messages is that he offers us not only his wisdom, but also the wisdom of the ages and sages. Where, we are driven to ask, does he find all those quotations and anecdotes? He cites not only Jewish tradition, but sources from classical Greece and Rome, from Elizabethan and Victorian England, from famous and obscure American writers; and his citations are always apt and memorable.

Perhaps the most important message of *Lessons for Living* is that every one of us has the capacity to act wisely and to increase the happiness in our lives.

No matter what fate may have in store for us, our lives can be rich with meaning, because previous generations have left us their wisdom and experience. Gifted interpreters of that wisdom and experience, such as Rabbi Greenberg, enable us to share and benefit from an uplifting religious tradition. Religion is a treasure which we need only reach out and claim; assuredly, we will be the richer for it.

A teacher of mine used to tell us: the spider creates only from within himself and the web he spins is sterile and deadly. The honeybee takes a little from this flower and a little from that flower, and the result is sweet and delicious. Let us remember this when we find ourselves sharing Rabbi Greenberg's stories and insights with others —as inevitably we will.

I rejoice that Rabbi Greenberg's comments and reflections are now available to us in this convenient format.

RABBI HAROLD S. KUSHNER
Natick, Mass.

Reflections on the
Weekly Bible Readings

"Don't Blame Me"

HE CAME TO SEE the marriage counsellor about his twenty-year-old marriage which was threatening to fall apart. He enumerated several things that had soured the relationship, and in each instance he put the blame on his wife. Finally, the counsellor asked him: "Do you think that the entire responsibility for your troubles rests with your wife?" He thought for a moment and then replied: "No, not really. She's only fifty percent to blame. The other fifty percent belongs to her mother."

This refusal to accept any personal responsibility for the sorry state of the marriage, this eagerness to blame others for what went wrong in his life is a fairly common human characteristic. The psychologists call it projection. Anna Russell, the British comedienne-singer, has a little lyric that tells how this face-saving mechanism works:

> "But now I'm happy; I have learned
> The lesson this has taught;
> That everything I do that's wrong
> Is someone else's fault."

The human tendency to avoid moral responsibility for misdeeds is scarcely a modern phenomenon. It is as old as man himself.

When Adam in the Garden of Eden eats from the forbidden tree, God confronts him with the accusing question: "Have you eaten from the tree that I commanded you not to eat?" Adam defends himself by saying: "The woman whom You gave me, she gave me of the tree and I did eat."

Notice what Adam is doing. He is dividing the blame equally between the Almighty and the woman. "The woman whom You gave me . . ." I didn't ask for her. She was Your idea and Your creation. "She gave me of the tree . . ." The eating was her idea not mine.

Now before we get the impression that evading moral responsibility is strictly a masculine affliction, we should read further into the Biblical incident. After Adam passes the moral buck to Eve, God asks her: "What is this that you have done?" Not to be outdone Eve replies: "The serpent beguiled me and I did eat."

The Torah doesn't report any conversation between the Almighty and the serpent on this matter. It would have been interesting to hear the serpent's excuse.

Projecting on to others the blame for our actions is one of our most persistent human traits. A newspaper item reported some of the explanations motorists gave to the Nevada police for accidents in which they were involved. A few choice samples follow:

"I pulled away from the side of the road, glanced at my mother-in-law and headed over the embankment."

"A pedestrian hit me and went under my car."

"This guy was all over the road. I had to swerve a number of times before I hit him."

Every age has its own Eves and its own serpents. In an earlier, less sophisticated age, when people believed in astrology, it was heavenly bodies which served as the Eves and the serpents. Shakespeare captured the buck-passing exceedingly well in the words of Edmund in "King Lear":

"This is the excellent foppery of the world that when we are sick in fortune—often the surfeit of our own behavior—we make guilty of our disasters the sun, the moon, the stars; as if we were villains by necessity, fools by heavenly compulsion . . ."

In our own times we are pictured as the passive victims of genes, reflexes, complexes. We are controlled by heredity or environment or both. Massive forces which you and I are impotent to control buffet us about and make us act as we do.

When Budget Director David Stockman made some indiscreet revelations to a journalist, the story was headlined on the cover of a respected magazine in these words: "Schizophrenia Made Stockman

Do It." How neat! Don't blame Stockman. The poor fellow is the captive of a dread disease. After the assassination attempt on President Reagan's life in 1981, the cover of *Time* magazine proclaimed the act to be "a moment of madness." Hinckley's jury apparently felt the same way and set him free. When a director of a large New York City bank was arrested for embezzling one million dollars, he said: "I don't know why I did it. Maybe a good psychiatrist can figure it out." Again, he was not to blame. Some mysterious forces were at work compelling him to steal. Let the psychiatrist discover them and hold them responsible. The mood of our time seems to be the old song: "Don't Blame Me."

But our tradition will not let us off the hook so easily. It looks upon us not as robots or puppets but as free moral agents who know the difference between right and wrong and who have the capacity to choose right over wrong.

To be sure, our biological inheritance, our childhood experiences, our environmental conditioning do exercise a vital influence upon us. These factors are real and powerful, but the human will is no less powerful.

We are not only shaped by our environment; we shape it. We are not only the creatures of circumstance; we are also the creators of circumstance.

Our genes may determine whether our eyes are blue or brown, but whether we look upon each other with cold indifference or warm compassion is for us to choose.

Our physical height may be biologically determined but our human stature we fashion ourselves.

Our environment determines the language we speak and the pronunciation we use, but whether our words are cruel or gentle, carping or comforting depends squarely upon us. Our passions, appetites and instincts are part of our animal equipment, but whether they rule us or we rule them is left for each of us to determine.

One of the hallmark verses of the Torah tells us: "I have set before you life and death, the blessing and the curse; choose life . . ."

It is only when we believe that there are indeed moral choices and that we have the power to make moral choices that we can truly live meaningful lives.

When Life Is Cheap

RECENTLY THERE WAS a court ruling that the use of home video recordings was against the law because the machines infringed on the copyrights of the producers of television programs. Moreover, according to the ruling, the manufacturers of these recorders and the stores that sold them could be sued for making them available to the consumer.

Shortly after the ruling was handed down, the *Philadelphia Inquirer* published a caustic cartoon by Conrad. In the center was a large video recorder. In the lower right-hand corner was a handgun. At the base of the cartoon was this question: "On which item have the courts ruled that manufacturers and retailers be held responsible for having supplied the equipment?"

This is a question to give us painful pause. Video recorders are subject to greater control than handguns, which are used in 30 murders every 24 hours in America. The cartoon also accuses us of the cardinal irreverence—putting property rights above human rights, holding things dear and life cheap.

According to the ancient Jewish Sages, this was precisely the sin of the builders of the Biblical Tower of Babel. When one of the laborers fell from a scaffold to his death, no one paid attention. But when one of the bricks fell down and smashed, there was great weeping and wailing. They, too, held things dear and life cheap. It was this perversion of values that provoked God and caused Him to "confuse their tongues" and to "scatter them over the face of the whole earth."

Quite obviously, the sin of the tower builders did not die with them. It is alive and doing its mischief among us. At least that's the way it appears to this observer. And it is not only the video recorders and handguns that I am thinking of.

What is one to think about the neutron bomb? Its very function strikes me as being obscene. It kills people but leaves buildings intact. I suppose that bombs are not to be faulted for lacking a sense of moral discrimination, but there is something inherently perverse in a bomb that respects property and demolishes people. Is this not the ultimate assault upon human dignity?

And what are we to make of this dreary statistic? The United States and the Soviet Union each has the equivalent of 30,000 pounds of TNT for every man, woman and child on the face of this earth! The only commodity available in such chilling abundance is the power to obliterate life.

We do not have in reserve 30,000 pounds of food, clothing, medicine or books for every human being. In 1960, there was a reserve stock of food grain sufficient for 102 days of world consumption; in 1980, there was enough only for 40 days.

Despite this ominous disparity between our expanding capacity to destroy life and our shrinking capacity to sustain it, we are now contemplating massive increases in appropriations for weapons of destruction and equally massive decreases in appropriations for human services.

It has been proposed that we increase defense spending to more than a quarter of a trillion dollars. Over the next five years $1.5 trillion will be put at the Pentagon's disposal.

These staggering sums will require painful cutbacks in old people's pensions and poor children's lunches. Food stamps to the needy will be drastically reduced. There will be less money available for education, child welfare, foster care, adoption assistance. Other programs to be victimized include alcohol and drug rehabilitation, health care, aid to the handicapped, legal aid to those who cannot afford to pay. The frigid breath of economy will also be felt by the arts and humanities, by parks, museums, opera, symphony orchestras, public television and radio.

In brief, all the proud hallmarks of a humane and civilized society will be offered on the altar of the illusory goal of military supremacy.

The words of the poet Lilith Lorraine seem to be pointing accusingly directly at us:

> "When planes outsoar the spirits, flying blind,
> When ships outsail the dreams that gave them birth,
> When towers dwarf the upward reaching mind,
> When wealth is mightier than simple worth—
> We almost hear the turning of a page,
> We almost know what every seraph knows,
> That somewhere on a universal stage,
> A tiresome play is drawing to its close."

It is not too late to re-examine our basic values and priorities. The drama of American democracy need not be "a tiresome play drawing to its close." It can be a continuing story of expanding human horizons, and deepening commitments to the true sources of our country's vigor and glory.

Every Day Is Examination Day

IN A TRIBUTE to Albert Einstein, George Bernard Shaw once drew a distinction between "empire builders" and "universe builders." Napoleon, he said, was an empire builder, but empires are notoriously perishable. Einstein was a universe builder whose discoveries would endure as long as people hungered for truth.

Another universe builder was Abraham, of whom we read in the early chapters of Genesis. It is to him we are indebted for the incandescent truth that one invisible God is the Creator of the universe and the Father of every human being.

This truth did not come cheap. The Bible tells us that "God tested Abraham." The Jewish Sages taught that Abraham was tested no fewer than ten times.

Again and again when a burden was laid upon him, when a risky assignment was given to him, when a luring temptation was placed before him, Abraham felt himself being tested. Each trial was an opportunity to demonstrate to himself and to God, the stuff of which he was made.

Is this the secret of his radiant life? Is this the attitude we need if our lives are to be the meaningful adventures we know they can be? Must we, too, learn to regard life as a classroom and every experience as a quiz whose purpose it is to determine not what we know but what we are?

In James Agee's sensitive posthumously published novel, *A Death*

In The Family, a father tries to comfort his daughter whose husband was killed in an auto accident. The unsophisticated father reveals genuine homespun wisdom and insight. He tells her that he realizes how little anyone can help her. She must work this thing out alone. He also points out "that nobody that ever lived is specially privileged; the axe can fall at any moment, on any neck, without any warning. . . . You've got to keep your mind off pitying your own rotten luck and setting up any kind of howl about it." He reassures her that she will come through this as millions like her have come through it before. And then the father says these words: "It's a kind of test, Mary, and it's the only kind that amounts to anything. When something rotten like this happens, then you have your choice. You start to really be alive or you start to die. That's all." Note well those words: "It's a kind of test, Mary."

Our Sages correctly observed: "There is no creature whom the Holy One, blessed be He, does not test." We are all tested. We are always tested. Whether we are aware of it or not, life is constantly springing little quizzes on us.

Every day is examination day. As husbands we are tested and as wives we are tested. As children we are tested and as parents we are tested. The doctor confronting his patient is having his dedication tested. The lawyer consulting with his client is having his integrity tested. The rabbi preparing his sermon, the writer at his desk, is each having his honesty tested. The teacher preparing a lesson is having his or her devotion tested. The businessman on the telephone, the carpenter building a shed, the mechanic under the car, the painter on the scaffold—each is having his character tested.

When a neighbor has been bruised our kindness is tested. When one has been blessed our generosity is tested. When we have been hurt our forgiveness is tested. When we have hurt our humility is tested. Trouble tests our courage. Temptation tests our strength. Friendship tests our loyalty. Failure tests our perseverance. Success tests our gratitude.

No day is free from its full quota of tests. Indeed the uses to which we put each day, the purposes to which we dedicate it, the deeds with which we fill it—constitute perhaps the supreme test of all. Not too long ago, an advertisement in the London *Times* read: "Some months to kill. Executive, 28, requires income for the assassination." To pass the daily quiz which the Father of all administers to us we must look upon time not as something to be killed but as something to be cherished. The prayer of the Psalmist is an excellent preparation for this test: "Teach us to number our days."

To look upon life as a test means to bring to it at every time the finest of which we are capable, to keep ourselves always in top moral condition, to realize the enormous possibilities for good or for ill inherent in each situation regardless of how unspectacular, or humdrum, or even ominous it may appear.

Ralph Waldo Emerson put this truth in striking words: "It is one of the illusions that the present hour is not the critical, decisive hour. Write it on your heart that every day is the best day of the year. No man has earned anything rightly until he knows that every day is doomsday. Today is a king in disguise. . . . Let us not be deceived, let us unmask the king as he passes."

The Unforgivable Error

ONE OF THE first lessons taught in Homiletics at the Jewish Theological Seminary is that a rabbi never reads simply for pleasure. A rabbi must always be wearing sermonic spectacles because ideas waiting to be preached lurk in the most unsuspected places. If Shakespeare could find "sermons in stones" why should we not be able to find sermons in the morning newspaper or even in a mystery story?

A case in point is one of Agatha Christie's tales. Her detective hero Hercule Poirot says to his good friend Captain Hastings: "It is your destiny to stand beside me and prevent me from committing the unforgivable error."

"What do you call the unforgivable error?" the captain asks.

Poirot answers: "Overlooking the obvious."

When we stop to reflect upon the detective's answer we realize that overlooking the obvious is indeed if not "the unforgivable error" at least a very widespread human error. In an age when we have walked on the moon and conducted space flights to explore planets hundreds of millions of miles away, our attention has been focused on distant horizons, while we too frequently overlook the crucial matters so close at hand.

But "the unforgivable error" of overlooking the obvious is not a product of the space age. This Torah portion talks of it long ago. There we find Hagar and her son Ishmael dying of thirst in the wilderness of Beer-Sheba. In despair she places her child under one of the shrubs and sits some distance away. "For she thought: 'I cannot look on as the child dies.' And sitting thus at a distance she wept loudly. . . . Then God opened her eyes and she saw a well of water; and she went and filled the bottle with water, and gave the lad drink."

Let us note carefully what the Torah tells us about Hagar's deliverance. God did not create a well in answer to her desperate prayers. The well had been there all along. Her source of salvation and survival was close at hand. What God did for Hagar was to open her eyes so that she saw the well, the obvious she had overlooked.

I often wish that God would do for us what He did for Hagar— simply open our eyes to the unnumbered glories that surround us, the manifold blessings which sustain us; His "miracles which attend us daily, morning, noon and night."

If only we could see the obvious, what an effective antidote that would be to our gnawing discontent, our insatiable ambitions, our quiet desperation, our restless nights, our parched days. The fly in the ointment gets all our attention while we remain unmindful of the ointment. So preoccupied are we with what we lack that we are unmindful of what we possess.

Helen Keller was most sensitive to this common human failing and there is a special poignancy to the words she wrote in *The World I Live In*. "I have walked with people whose eyes are full of light but who see nothing in woods, sea or sky, nothing in the city street, nothing in books. . . .

"It were far better to sail forever in the night of blindness with sense and feeling and mind than to be thus content with the mere act of seeing.

"They have the sunset, the morning skies, the purple of distant hills, yet their souls voyage through this enchanted world with nothing but a barren stare."

A few years ago the famous choreographer Agnes de Mille suffered a serious illness and after a long hard road to recovery she wrote about what illness had taught her. "I had a destroyed body," she wrote, "but I got a new way of looking at things. . . . My life pattern had been broken, the habits smashed. . . . The fight back to health has brought me a new sense of awareness. I think it's very invigorating to call a sharp halt to life and pay attention to what's going on and what we are doing. I believe we could learn a great deal and could take joy and power in matters which usually go totally unnoticed."

When we overlook the obvious we not only miss the beauty and the blessings which are close at hand, we also lose sight of the opportunities for fulfillment which we already possess. How often we delude ourselves into believing that if only circumstances were different, if we lived elsewhere, if we had a different environment, O how happy we could be. When we get into the mood of "if only" we would do well to ask ourselves whether we are not making the unforgivable error.

Among the Hasidim they tell the tale of poor Rabbi Eizik of Cracow. He had a recurring dream that under the bridge which leads to the king's palace in Prague there was a great treasure. If he would journey there and dig he need never know poverty any more.

Rabbi Eizik made the journey, found the bridge but he did not dare to try to dig because the bridge was guarded day and night. Finally the guard who had observed him asked what he was doing all this time near the bridge. Rabbi Eizik told him of the dream which had brought him here.

Whereupon the guard burst into laughter. "You have faith in dreams! If I believed in dreams I would have had to go to Cracow, because long ago I dreamed that there was a treasure buried beneath the kitchen stove of some Jew named Rabbi Eizik."

Rabbi Eizik took his shovel, returned home and dug up the treasure beneath his own stove. With the money he built a *Shul* which they called *Rabbi Eizik's Shul*.

L'ḥayyim—To Life!

THE TITLE OF this *Sidrah* contrasts sharply with its opening theme. The first portion of the Torah reading (Gen. 23) speaks of the death of the first Jewish mother, Sarah, Abraham's weeping and mourning for her, and then her burial. But despite its preoccupation with Sarah's death, the *Sidrah* bears the title "*Hayyei Sarah*," "The *Life* of Sarah."

Nor is this the only time we find in the Torah a *Sidrah* whose title is in such striking contrast to its contents. The last Torah portion in Genesis begins with a deathbed scene. The Patriarch Jacob is taking final leave of his family. He blesses his grandchildren and his children. "And when Jacob finished charging his sons, he gathered up his feet into the bed, and died, and he was gathered unto his people" (Gen. 49:33).

The Torah then describes Jacob's burial and the period of mourning which both preceded and followed it.

What is the title of this *Sidrah*? "*Vayehi*"—"And He *Lived*."

It would appear that in these two titles of Torah portions dealing with death, our tradition wanted to soften the pain of bereavement by focusing on life. When a loved one dies we are overwhelmed by the awareness of what death has taken from us. At such a time our tradition would have us remember also what that life has left with us.

Death can only take from us what might have been. It cannot take from us what has already been. It cannot rob us of our past. The days and years we shared, the common adventures and joys, the "little, nameless acts of kindness and of love"—all these are part of the ineradicable record. Death has no dominion over them.

We who have lost loved ones know with unwavering certainty that for us our loved ones always remain living presences. Hans Zinsser went even further when he wrote: "At times the dead are closer to us than the living, and the wisdom and affection of the past stretch blessing hands over our lives, projecting a guardian care out of the shadows and helping us over hard places. For there are certain kinds of love that few but the very wise understand until they have become memories."

As we study human reactions to sorrow we are struck by the frequency with which people who were so grievously impoverished by a death could yet find strength to express gratitude for that life.

Listen to the Chicago born Hebrew poet Reuben Grossman whose son Noam studied at the Hebrew University, became an officer in the Haganah and was killed in Israel's War of Independence. After his son's death, the poet changed his name to Avinoam which in Hebrew means "father of Noam." At the end of the *Shivah*, the father wrote a poem entitled: "Therefore, We Thank You God."

In it he lists all the things in Noam's life for which he feels "thanks pouring from the wound of our heart." Among them are:

> "For pleasant years,
> For one and twenty years
> Wherein You honoured us with him and lent him us,
> For his steps walking humbly by our side on the little isle of life:
> Years sown with the peace of his being,
> When like a gliding swan he made his way erect with grace;
> Years shining with smiles
> Which like sunrays he spread around him,
> With good-hearted whispers, pardons by concession and
> understanding,
> Years shining with the light of his two eyes,
> Where dreams yearned, mingled with the sorrow of fate,
> Having a pure look and upright before God and man.
> For this little gift,
> For twenty-one full years of life You gave him and us,
> We thank you. . . ."

Another bereaved father who found the strength to express gratitude amidst his grief was the celebrated American newspaper editor William Allen White. In reply to a friend who wrote him a condolence letter upon the death of his daughter Mary, White wrote a most moving and poignant letter of appreciation which he concluded with these words:

"Mrs. White and I are standing on our feet, realizing that the loss is heavy and the blow is hard, but not beating our hands against the bars and asking why. On our books Mary is a net gain. She was worth so much more than she cost, and she left so much more behind than she took away that we are flooded with joyous memories and cannot question either the goodness of God or the general decency of man."

When our tradition put the stamp of life on chapters dealing with death it also pointed perhaps to the powerful truth that ultimately it is not death but life that has the last word. The soul is imperishable and "the grave is not its goal." The souls of our loved ones, like our own, came from the great Source of Life and flow back into the eternal stream after our earthly pilgrimage is ended.

The pain of parting is mitigated by our faith in a divine providence which permits no life to be utterly destroyed. We are sustained by "the Soul's invincible surmise." This was the faith burst forth out of Emerson after the death of his young son: "What is excellent, as God lives, is permanent."

Perhaps all of Jewish wisdom in this matter is captured in the common practice we have all seen. Upon returning from the cemetery after a burial, we take a little whiskey and before we drink it we raise the glass and say: *"L'hayyim"*—to life!

There Are No Sure Bets

IT IS TOLD of one student of child behavior that he frequently delivered a lecture entitled, "Ten Commandments For Parents." He married and became a father. He changed the title of his lecture to "Ten Hints For Parents." A second child was born and the lecture title became "Some Suggestions for Parents." When a third child arrived the lecturer stopped lecturing.

Our "expert" was not the first authority to discover that many a lovely theory on child rearing is often assaulted by a gang of brutal facts. What works for one child may not work for another and whether it works or not we may not know until long after we have done parenting. Children are unpredictable. We never know how far up the wall they will drive us.

An old Yiddish adage assures us that "the apple doesn't fall far from the tree." This bit of folk wisdom is supposed to guarantee the strongest resemblance in personality and character traits between parents and children. But who cannot testify out of personal observation that often the distance that separates the apple from the tree is quite large and, what is more, often the apples from the same tree are quite unlike each other.

The late Gershom Scholem, an outstanding authority on Jewish mysticism and kabbalah, was one of four brothers. One of them was attracted to no ideals or movements. One became a right-wing German nationalist. A third, turned communist, was a member of the Reichstag and was killed by the Nazis in Buchenwald. Gershom himself devoted his life to studying and teaching our heritage. Reflecting why the four brothers should have followed such divergent paths, Gershom confesses that he has no answer. "There are personal decisions whose 'secrets' no one knows."

A more striking instance of apples from the same tree which were quite unlike each other is found in this Torah portion. There we read of the twin brothers Jacob and Esau. They emerge from the same womb, at the same time, are nurtured in the same home by the same parents, and yet they are so strikingly different in temperament, in outlook, in their life's values.

Esau is a hunter, the rugged man of the outdoors, a physical person, sensuous, self-indulgent. Jacob is turned inward, sensitive to things of the mind and spirit, preferring the quiet life.

Two brothers, twins, so close together at birth, so far apart in their maturity. And a wall of hatred separated them.

The dramatically different personalities of the twin brothers is mirrored in a remarkable phenomenon in nature. At one point in the Rocky Mountains some 10,000 feet above sea level, there are two streams of water which run alongside each other but in opposite directions. One of them moves toward the East and ultimately empties into the Gulf of Mexico. The other stream flows toward the West and finally empties into the Pacific Ocean. And there is a big range of mountains between them.

What is the point of all this? The point is that each child is a mystery, each child is unique, totally unlike any other child that was ever born or will ever be born. With all the best intentions and the most devoted care and nurturing, parents can accomplish only so much with a child.

There was a time when the behavioral psychologists convinced us that the newborn infant is like a blank sheet of paper waiting for the parents to write on it. Today we know better.

The child comes into the world with its basic temperament determined by the wholly accidental combination of millions of genes which carry not only the traits of its parents but also of ancestors long forgotten. These are the true "designer genes." And no two children can be expected to be alike. That is why one authority tells us that bringing up children by the book is well enough provided we keep in mind that we need a different book for each child.

One long-suffering wife confided to a good friend, "My husband has changed his faith. He no longer believes he is God." So often we strike a pose of infallibility, handing down pronouncements and opinions as though they were carved at Sinai in stone together with the original tablets. We pretend to know all there is to know about everything while we suppress the haunting suspicion that we may indeed be mistaken and the certainty that what we don't know exceeds by far the little we do know.

One successful businessman put on his office wall in bold letters the sobering words, "I may be wrong." That may have been the reason for his success; his willingness to learn from others, his ability to keep his mind open to a new idea, a different approach. His motto was a free translation of Jacob's rhetorical question, "Am I in the place of God?"

Jacob's question is also good for our sanity. When we recognize our human limitations we stop demanding perfection of ourselves. We are not 100 percent parents, we are not 100 percent mates, we are not 100 percent children. And we ought to stop tormenting ourselves, as we so frequently do, for falling short of perfection in one or all of the myriad relationships in which we are involved. Often we must make painful choices between our mates and our parents, our parents and our children, and we cannot possibly satisfy all.

When we acknowledge the built-in limitations of the human condition we also avoid the destructive tendency to blame ourselves when children do not turn out exactly as we had hoped. Deluded by a sense of omnipotence we succumb to the illusion that when kids go wrong it is all our fault. We have done it to them. We forget the many other factors that go into the making and the shaping of a child—the genes of generations past, the environment, the TV, the friends on the street, the teachers in the classroom, the characters the child encounters in books. These are only some of the multitude of forces at work, and while no parent has the right to abdicate responsibility, neither has the parent the right to arrogate unto himself the feeling of invincibility.

Emerson said there is a crack in everything that God has made. Perfection is beyond human reach. Jacob captured this truth in his question, "Am I in the place of God?"

In a letter to William James, Justice Holmes wrote, "The great act of faith is when a man decides he is not God." When we realize that we are not God we have a better chance of becoming human.

Coming Home

AT VACATION TIME the freeway near the University of California in Berkeley is lined with students trying to hitch rides home. The students usually display large signs with their destinations printed in bold letters. Despite the intense competition for rides, one student got a lift almost as soon as he held up his sign. It said: "Mom's waiting."

That young man exploited one of our most profound and most enduring loves—the love of home. The mere mention of the word evokes an almost mystic reverence and misty nostalgia. Home is one of the largest words in our emotional vocabulary.

Home is Mom waiting, home is comfort when bruised, home is sorrow eased and joy enlarged, home is childhood and growing up, home is hot food and warm beds, snow etching faces on the window and the morning sun announcing the time to get up. "Home," as Robert Frost said, "is the place where, when you have to go there, they have to take you in."

The homing instinct in birds has been well documented. In *The Territorial Imperative*, Robert Ardrey tells about a bird known as the Manx Shearwater from Skokholm Island off the Coast of Wales. A Cambridge scientist transported it by airplane from its native habitat to Harvard University. There is was tagged and released. The Shearwater was back in its burrow on Skokholm Island twelve and one half days later. The bird had flown 3050 miles covering an average of 244 miles per day!

Is there also a homing instinct in human beings? Every indication points to its existence. How else can we explain the opening passage of this *Sidrah* where we find Jacob returning home after an absence of some twenty years? After all, home for Jacob means facing his brother Esau who had vowed to kill him. That is why Jacob fled from his home in the first place. Coming home means not only jeopardizing his own life but also the lives of his wives and children. Despite the awesome risk of coming home Jacob throws all caution aside and faces homeward. Why? Was it because the homing instinct in him is too strong to be denied?

Was it also the homing instinct that kept alive in our people the love for *Eretz Yisrael* through the long, hard centuries down the drafty corridors of history? Wherever we traveled we took with us the hope for return to the land of our origins. We echoed that hope in our daily prayers, and "home" was the direction we faced when we offered those prayers.

In July of 1967, a group of Conservative rabbis and their wives arrived in Israel on a pilgrimage. Avraham Fradkin greeted them with these words: "Welcome to Israel! Welcome home!" Avraham was right. Israel is the place where a Jew feels at home even though he has never been there before. There is within us a latent spark that bursts into a warming flame upon contact with this niggardly piece of geography. Israel is many things to many peoples and faiths. But to the Jew alone it is home, and it is the homing instinct that has brought us back to our ancestral land.

The homing instinct works upon Jews in other ways. It has helped to bring many an alienated Jew back to his people. Former Supreme Court Justice Felix Frankfurter was for a brief time active in Zionism under the influence of Louis D. Brandeis. For years before his death however he had virtually no association with Jewish life. As for the Jewish religion, he claimed to have left the Synagogue at the age of 15, never to return.

But when he was ailing in his advanced years he instructed a good friend, Garson Kanin, about his own funeral arrangements. He asked that one of the participants in the funeral service be a certain close friend "who is also a practicing Orthodox Jew. He knows Hebrew perfectly well and will know exactly what to say."

"Do you mean a prayer of some sort?"

"Well, of course, you nut, what else would he say in Hebrew?"

"Then you mean the Kaddish?"

"Oh, I don't know and neither do you, but he'll know and he'll do it beautifully. Let me explain. I came into the world a Jew; I think it is fitting that I should leave as a Jew. I don't want to be one of those pretenders and turn my back on a great and noble heritage."

And there is still another way that the homing instinct affects us. It is suggested by our reaction to E.T. Adults no less than children were taken by this ugly extra-terrestrial little creature whose vocabulary consists of a single word—"home." There is a deep sadness in his watery eyes as he points his bony finger toward the heavens indicating the source of his distress—home-sickness. Why did he touch us so? Is it because, like E.T., we too are longing for home? Homesickness can afflict even those of us who are secure in our own terrestrial homes.

In "The Bella Lingua," John Cheever offers a revealing insight into our human condition. One of his characters says: "Fifty percent of the people in the world are homesick all the time. . . . You don't really long for another country. You long for something in yourself that you don't have, or haven't been able to find."

What is this something for which we long in our homesickness even when we are at home? The poet Wordsworth gave us a clue to our malaise when he said "trailing clouds of glory we come, from God who is our home." The longing, the yearning that we can't define is for the very source of our being, God.

Dr. Louis Finkelstein has spoken directly to this theme. Despite all our unprecedented affluence, he noted, there is among us restlessness, confusion, increasing neuroses and general unhappiness.

"Living in a gilded palace, as it were, we are still miserable, for we are essentially orphans, having lost that most precious of all values in life, the sense of the Fatherhood of God. . . .

"More than ever then do we become homesick; homesick not for our houses or for our countries, but homesick for the universal Parent of all of us, for that deep affection which is at the heart of the universe itself, for the mercy of God. . . ."

Dr. Finkelstein invites us to come home. It's an invitation we would be wise to accept.

Forgive Us Our Virtues

FIFTY YEARS ago Vardis Fisher wrote a novel with the ironic title *Forgive Us Our Virtues*. It is a title calculated to puncture the balloon of moral smugness. It reminds us of the harm we so often inflict with the best of intentions and with the noblest of instincts.

A poignant illustration of this truth is found in this *Sidrah*. It tells of the bitter feelings that tore apart Jacob's family—a family riddled by gossip, envy and hatred. Only narrowly do Joseph's brothers avoid killing him and instead they sell him into slavery. Then they practice the cruelest of all deceptions, they convince Jacob that Joseph is dead.

What was it that so terribly splintered this family? Love! Yes, a father's discriminating love. Jacob, the Torah tells us, "loved Joseph more than all his children. . . . and he made him a coat of many colors. And when his brothers saw that their father loved him more than all his brothers, they hated him, and could not speak peaceably to him" (Gen. 27:3-4).

Had Jacob realized the destructive power of his misplaced love, perhaps he might have prayed: "Forgive us our virtues."

One of the distressing truths about human nature is that there is no virtue that cannot be turned into a vice, no quality which is immune to corruption.

Surely, we would say, fervent religious zeal is a laudable virtue. And yet anyone who has read Jewish history knows how exorbitant has been the price we have paid for the religious zeal of those who sought to convert us to their faith. They resorted to all manner of coercion and torture and bribery to "persuade" us and when these failed, when they could not win our souls, they often destroyed our bodies or expelled us from countries we had served faithfully and enriched abundantly with our industry and our genius.

Did any of our tormentors in a mood of repentance ever pause to pray: "Forgive us our virtues"?

As we come a little closer to home and pause to examine our own lives, we find so many sins which we commit with the best of intentions.

Surely our love for our children is a noble virtue. But when we see parents express this love by trying to solve all their children's problems, permitting them to carry no burdens, take no risks, make no decisions, shoulder no responsibility, submit to no discipline; when we see fathers so obsessed with providing for their family's exaggerated security needs that they sacrifice their health, their leisure and sometimes even their integrity, we should be moved to pray: "Forgive us our virtues."

Surely tolerance is a virtue. But when we become tolerant of the intolerable, when we accept passively circumstances and conditions which should fill us with flaming protest and hot indignation, when we remain calmly indifferent to public corruption and betrayal, surely it is time to pray: "Forgive us our virtues."

Righteousness too easily degenerates into self-righteousness. Candor is frequently a mask for cruelty. Caution can become timidity. Freedom can turn into license. Self-confidence can become arrogance. Humility can become servility. Curiosity makes a good scientist but a bad neighbor.

In Macaulay's "Oliver Goldsmith" we see how easily virtue can turn into fault. "In truth, there was in his character much to love but very little to respect. His heart was soft even to weakness; he was so generous that he quite forgot to be just; he forgave injuries so readily that he might be said to invite them; and he was so liberal to beggars that he had nothing left for his tailor and his butcher."

Small wonder then that a keen observer of the mysterious workings of human nature has written: "The enterprise of living means reckoning with the ravages of virtue as well as those of vice. The evil in the world comes not only from unbridled wrong but also from unbridled good." From time to time we might pause to consider whether we should pray: Forgive us our virtues.

We Can't Live on Miracles

A POPULAR folk saying in Israel today is that if you don't believe in miracles you're not a realist. Believing in miracles comes naturally to the descendants of a people whose entire existence has been one continuous miracle, whose rebirth out of the ashes of the Holocaust was one of history's most spectacular miracles.

But there is another piece of folk wisdom which comes in the form of a question and answer. Why do we eat latkes on Hanukkah? Because on miracles alone you can't live. Israel's first president, Chaim Weizmann, was one of the most prominent contributors to its rebirth, and he spoke out of the depths of personal experience when he said: "Miracles sometimes occur but one has to work terribly hard for them."

He was cautioning us against believing in miracles too much, against depending upon them so heavily that we forget that so many of God's miracles are man made, that there is an enormous human component that goes into the making of a miracle.

Hanukkah itself provides a dramatic illustration of this truth. The word itself means "dedication" and at the heart of the festival is the joy of the rededication of the Temple in Jerusalem after the incredible victory of the vastly outnumbered Maccabees over the Syrians who had defiled it. But the rededication of the Temple would have been impossible if there had not been a powerful dedication on the part of the Jewish people to their heritage and their faith.

If the truth be told, not all Jews at that time had this sense of dedication. There were in fact the Hellenists who were quite content to throw in the *Tallit*. They adopted the Greek gods, the Greek language, Greek sports, Greek modes of dress, Greek names. Hebrew was neglected. The Sabbath and Jewish festivals were gradually replaced by pagan observances. Some of the Hellenists even underwent a painful surgical procedure to undo the circumcision so that they might appear in the public arena in the nude!

Had these Hellenists prevailed there would have been no resistance, no war, no Temple, no Jewish religion, no miracle. But because there were enough Jews who cared enough about preserving Judaism, their distinctive way of life, and their own spiritual identity, they decided that "they would rather fight than switch." Without their own fierce dedication there would have been no Temple dedication. Yes, miracles sometimes happen but we have to work hard to make them happen.

This is a truth worth pondering. People often say they don't believe in miracles, and yet their behavior, or lack of it, indicates that they believe in miracles too much. They expect good things to happen without any effort on their part. No toil, no travail, no sacrifice, no surrender of comfort or leisure or pleasure; just relying on miracles to happen.

Some time ago, there was a popular song which assured us that "wishing will make it so." Our own experience raises serious doubt about that glib optimism. A wish-bone rarely accomplishes a thing until it is joined to the back-bone and the finger-bone.

Long ago our Sages, who surely could not be accused of lacking faith in God, warned us: "We may not rely on miracles." They knew that wishing will not make it so unless we are prepared to work with God to translate those wishes into reality, those desires into deeds.

A pupil once asked his rabbi why the Almighty endowed man with skepticism. "After all," he asked, "we have been taught that everything He created has some beneficial purpose, but what possible purpose could skepticism serve? It only leads to doubt and denial of faith."

The rabbi was ready with his answer. "There are times," he answered, "when it is better not to have too much faith in the Almighty. When a poor man comes to you for help because he and his children are hungry, do not send him away with the assurance that the *Ribbono Shel Olam* (Master of the Universe) will perform some miracle for him. That is when you use your skepticism. Act independently. You help the poor man yourself."

Let's not depend on miracles.

If we want Israel to be strong, secure and safe, what are we doing to make that wish come true?

If we want our children to be comfortable in their Jewishness, proud of their past and committed to its future, what are we doing to make that wish come true?

If we want the Jewish home to fulfill its historic role of shaping Jewish values and transmitting Jewish teachings, what are we doing to make that wish come true?

If we want the name Jew to stand for honesty, integrity and generosity, what are we doing to make that wish come true?

If we want creative Jewish survival to continue into the uncharted future, what are we doing to make that wish come true?

The court philosopher, we are told, had just completed his lecture on miracles, and after the applause ended the king turned to him with the challenge: "Show me a miracle." The philosopher reflected briefly and answered: "Sire, the Jews."

Jewish survival in the face of the most monstrous odds and towering threats has indeed been a massive miracle. The real miracle that we celebrate on Hanukkah is not the tiny cruse of oil that lasted so much longer than expected. The fact that we are still celebrating Hanukkah twenty-one and a half centuries later—that is the miracle. But that miracle was not made possible by casual Jews. Casual Jews too easily become Jewish casualties. In every age the miracle was renewed by the dedication, devotion and sacrificial love of men and women who cared enough to give their very best.

So at Hanukkah time, it's quite all right to believe in miracles, but let the latke remind us, that on miracles alone you can't live.

Which Shall We Choose to Remember?

A KEEN STUDENT of human behavior, George Halifax, has correctly said: "Could we know what men are most apt to remember we might know what they are most apt to do."

A vivid illustration of this truth is found in this *Sidrah*. Joseph is facing a memory problem in one of the most dramatic moments in his eventful life. The moment occurs when Joseph, who had been sold by his brothers into slavery, now finds these brothers before him. But now he has become the regent of Egypt and his brothers, driven by famine, appear before him for food. Joseph has them at his mercy. He can do with them as he wills. But what will he do? His problem is fundamentally one of memory. What should he remember?

He can remember how they maltreated him, cast him into the pit where he might have been left to perish had not an Ishmaelite caravan fortuitously appeared, how they coldly traded him away as if he were no more than a piece of sheepskin or a measure of corn. Or he can remember how he, the young Joseph, had provoked them, how he had brought tales of malice about them back to his father, how he had taunted them with his dreams of his destined domination over them. He can either remember the wrong he suffered or the wrong he inflicted. He can either exact vengeance or make amends. Which experience shall he remember?

This problem is not easily solved. Instinctively, Joseph appears ready to exact vengeance. In a variety of subtle ways he torments his brothers, worries them and hurls accusations against them. All this, however, is but the prelude which leads up to the climax—the moment when Joseph reveals himself to his brothers. When that moment arrives Joseph emerges in heroic stature. He has chosen to forget his brothers' misconduct and to make amends for his own.

When he notices the fear that registers on their faces he tells them: "Be not angry with yourselves that you sold me here, for God sent me before you to be a preserver of life. It was not you but God who sent me here." He then goes on to assure them that he will make arrangements for them and their families to live in Egypt where he will provide for them all. In this way does Joseph solve his personal memory problem.

Each of us at one time or another has to draw up a memory balance sheet. What shall we try to remember and what shall we try to forget?

We must try to forget those things which if remembered would bring out our unworthy traits. We must try to remember those things which if forgotten would suppress our nobler instincts.

Some among us have permitted ties of family and friendship to be broken. There was an unpleasant scene, a heated exchange of words, an explosive moment. We chose to remember that moment while we forgot all the unnumbered pleasant moments of family loyalty and warmth of friendship. Would it not be much wiser now if we forgot the hurt and remembered only the love?

All of us have suffered wrongs and inflicted them. Too often we recall the instances when we were the victims; we forget those where we were the offenders. Were it not wiser to reverse our memory systems—consign the wrong suffered to oblivion and repair, where time yet permits, the wrong inflicted?

All too often we remember with bitterness the unfulfilled promises made to us but we calmly forget the pledge we made and did not honor, the resolve we made and did not keep, the word we gave and did not fulfill. Were it not better that we forgot the first and remembered the second?

None among us has not been both benefactor and beneficiary. We have benefitted others to be sure, but in more instances than we normally care to remember we have also reaped the harvest of another's kindness, another's generosity, another's sacrifice. If we enjoy the blessings of health, freedom, democracy, Judaism, it is because others have paid for these, our possessions, with their lives and their blood. Shall the little kindnesses we have shown make us haughty when there is so much that we have inherited which should make us profoundly grateful and humble?

Every day we see about us evidence of human pettiness, greed, self-centeredness. But if we observe carefully we also see human nobility, generosity, self-surrender and genuine religious conviction and action. The cynic remembers only man's faults—that is why he remains a cynic. The wise man remembers his brother's virtues. Which shall we choose to remember?

In making our choice let us remember that we shall be what we remember. Our memories will mold our action and what others will remember of us will be determined by what we choose to remember.

Where There's a Will

IN HIS "King Richard II," Shakespeare tells us that:

> "The tongues of dying men
> Enforce attention, like deep harmony:
> When words are scarce, they're seldom spent in vain;
> For they breathe truth that breathe their words in pain."

The last *Sidrah* of the Book of Genesis begins with the final hours in the life of Jacob who gathers together his children and grand-children to give to each in turn a parting word of blessing or admonition. Jacob speaks not a word about his worldly goods or possessions. He wants to leave to each of his children a measure of the wisdom life has taught him. He speaks not of valuables but of values.

We meet another dying man in the *Haftarah* of this Shabbat. Here we find David transmitting his "legacy of intangibles" (to use Stephen Vincent Benet's phrase) to his son Solomon, his successor to the throne.

We hear many "tongues of dying men" in the Talmud which recorded the last words of a number of the ancient Sages. Thus we read that when Rabbi Yohanan ben Zakkai became mortally ill, his pupils came to visit him and they asked him for his blessing. Where-upon he said to them: "May you fear heaven as you fear man."

"Is that all?" they asked. "Are we not obliged to fear God *more* than we fear man?"

"Indeed, we are," answered the master. "But I would be content if your fear of God would be only as great as your fear of man. When a person is about to commit a wrong he hopes no person sees him. If he were equally afraid of God who sees all, he would not sin."

The examples of the Biblical heroes and Talmudic Sages inspired successive generations of Jews to leave behind the moral and ethical instruction they wished their surviving loved ones to hold dear. So widespread did this practice become that in 1926 Israel Abrahams published two volumes entitled "Hebrew Ethical Wills" (Jewish Publication Society, paperback 1979).

In recent years I have come upon additional contemporary ethical wills which are worth our attention. I have selected three of them:

The first is from the Yiddish novelist Sholom Aleichem, which incidentally was read into the *Congressional Record*. A portion follows:

"Wherever I die I should be laid to rest not among the aristocrats, the elite, the rich, but rather among the plain people, the toilers, the common folk, so that the tombstone that will be placed on my grave will grace the simple graves about me, and the simple graves will adorn my tombstone even as the plain people have, during my life, beatified their folk writer . . .

" . . . at the annual recurrence of the day of my passing, my family and good friends generally should gather and read my will, and also select one of my stories, of the very merry ones, and recite it in whatever language is more intelligible to them; and let my name be recalled by them with laughter rather than not be remembered at all . . .

"My last wish and my prayer to my children: Take good care of Mother, grace her age, sweeten her bitter life, heal her broken heart; not to weep for me, on the contrary, to remember me with joy. And most importantly, live in peace together, bear no hatred for one another, help each other in bad times, think occasionally of the other members of the family, take pity on the poor, and when circumstances permit pay my debts, if there be such. Children, bear with honor my hard-earned Jewish name, and may God in Heaven sustain you ever. Amen."

Shortly before his untimely death in 1980 Sam Levenson, the beloved comedian, drew up his "Ethical Will and Testament," addressed to his grandchildren. It read in part:

"I leave you my unpaid debts. They are my greatest assets. Everything I own, I owe.

"To America I owe a debt for the opportunity it gave me to be free and to be me.

"To my parents I owe America. They gave it to me and I leave it to you. Take good care of it.

"To the Biblical tradition I owe the belief that man does not live by bread alone nor does he live alone at all. This is also the democratic tradition. Preserve it.

"I leave you everything I had in my lifetime; a good family, respect for learning, compassion for my fellow men, and some four-letter words for all occasions. Words like help, give, care, feel and love.

"I leave you the years I should like to have lived so that I might possibly see whether your generation will bring more love and peace to the world than ours did. I not only hope you will, I pray that you will."

The third will was left by Tzeeyon Chakmon, a 20-year-old Israeli paratrooper, the son of immigrants from Tripoli who had lost two young children from kidney disease. Because of this double tragedy, Tzeeyon was exempt from military service. But he volunteered for the army and then volunteered for a treacherous mission in 1980 to root out a terrorist nest in Southern Lebanon.

All Israeli soldiers are required to write letters home before leaving on a dangerous mission. When they return safely they tear up their letters. Tzeeyon did not return and this was the letter his parents received:

"In a short while I will be carrying out something that may determine my life. I know that it is difficult for you to accept what I am doing. But, I feel that it is my duty to do this. I do it for my country [Israel] and if I did not do it, one of my friends would have to do it. However, since I was selected for this task, there is no reason why I should refuse.

"I don't want to make this note too long. I just want you to understand me and see my actions in the right perspective, despite what happened in our family. Nevertheless, I fervently hope that I will continue to see you and be with you all my life. [Signed] Your son who loves you very very much—Tzeeyon."

The tradition of drawing up an ethical will is eminently worth perpetuating. No lawyer can do this for us. This is a do-it-yourself privilege. And where there is a will there is a way of life.

Growing Up and Growing Out

SEVERAL YEARS AGO a comedian who is Jewish was asked in a radio interview how he explains the astronomical sums American Jews contribute annually to their various charities. "Well," he answered, posing as the authority he obviously was not, "first you have to start with 2,000 years of persecution."

Not quite. First you have to start with 3,000 years of indoctrination.

Very early in our history we were taught that the hallmark of a Jew is a profound feeling of concern for the welfare of other Jews. One of the most striking illustrations of this lesson is found in the opening chapters of the Book of Exodus:

"And Moses grew up and he went out to his brothers and saw their burdens" (Ex. 2:11).

It would have been so natural, so understandable and oh so very practical had Moses chosen not to notice his brothers' travail, to claim no kinship with these degraded slaves. How tempting it must have been to cling to the security, the delights, the prerogatives of the royal palace in which his life was so snugly upholstered. But had Moses done so, God would not have noticed him and history would not have remembered him.

The whole course of human events was radically altered because in a decisive moment, an obscure foundling of a condemned people threw off the anonymity and the protection of Pharaoh's palace and "went out to his brothers and saw their burdens."

From that day to our very own, a crucial index of Jewish maturity is the ability to go out to our brothers and be sensitive to their burdens.

Two Chelmite "philosophers," not especially noted for their sophistication, were engaged in a profound discussion: How does one grow, from the feet up or from the head down?

Said the first: "From the feet up, of course. Last year I bought my son a new suit for his Bar Mitzvah and at that time the pants were just the right length. Now, the pants just reach his ankles. That proves that people grow from the feet up."

"Fool," snapped the second philosopher. "It's obvious that people grow from the head down. If you see a group of soldiers marching all their feet are on the same level. But if you look at their heads you will see that they are at different heights. That proves that people grow from the head down."

Both Chelmites were wrong. We grow neither from the bottom up nor from the top down. Genuine growth is from the inside out. The truest measure of our growth is the ability to go out to our brothers and become aware of their burdens.

When God measures us He puts the tape around the heart.

All growth is difficult. Our Sages tell us that no blade of grass grows except for an angel which stands over it and commands: "Grow!"

We are born selfish. To the infant the whole world exists for one supreme purpose—to minister to his needs. Growing up is the slow, painful process of learning that we are here not to be ministered to, but to minister; not to be served, but to serve; not to be fed but to feed; not to be imprisoned within ourselves, but to go out to our brothers.

But we are afraid to venture out. Seeing brothers gives them a claim over us. It is easier not to notice them, to acknowledge no kinship with them.

An eight-year-old unintentionally gave expression to this philosophy of evasion. During a Consecration Service, a rabbi addressed a youngster who bore the name of one of Jacob's sons, and the rabbi expressed the hope that the young fellow "would live a life of dedication to your brothers of the House of Israel." Without batting an eyelash, the youngster replied at the top of his voice: "I ain't got no brothers."

We can only hope that when that young fellow grows up he will discover that he does indeed "got" brothers, that he is intimately related to them by a thousand bonds of kinship, fate and loyalty, and that to the extent that he goes out to them will he fulfill his fundamental duty as a Jew and his fundamental need as a human being.

The act of giving is simultaneously an act of receiving. The benefactor is also the beneficiary. To give is to become enriched.

As we feed, we are fed. As we give, we receive. As we lift, we are raised. As we go out of ourselves into something bigger than ourselves, we become bigger in the process and we provide the most nourishing sustenance our craving hearts demand.

"Help your brother's boat across the river and lo, your own has reached the shore."

Reluctant Actors

A STORY the youngsters tell deals with the crossing of the sea by the Israelites as they fled Egypt. Seven-year-old David returns from religious school and is asked by his grandfather what he learned in *Heder*. Whereupon the pride of his life tells his *Zeyde* the following:

"As the Jews were running away from Egypt, Pharaoh and his army decided to bring them back and so he began to chase after them. When the Jews came to the sea, Moses called in the engineers who laid down pontoon bridges for his people to cross over. As soon as they reached the other side, Moses called in the Air Force who strafed and bombed the Egyptians and wiped them out."

The *Zeyde* could scarcely believe his ears. "Is this what they taught you in *Heder*?" he asked in amazement.

"Grandpa," said David, "if I told you the story as my teacher told it, you would never believe it."

The story of the Exodus even without the miracle at the sea is altogether an unbelievable story. A more unlikely drama would be hard to imagine. The three principal characters in the scenario are Moses, Pharaoh and the Israelites. And each is an unwilling participant reluctant to play the assigned role.

First there is Moses. When the Almighty appears to him with the announcement that He has heard the groanings of the Israelites, seen their suffering, and has determined to liberate them, He asks Moses to appeal to Pharaoh to let the people go. Moses protests his total unfitness for this impossible mission. "O Lord, I am not a man of words, neither in the past nor since You spoke to Your servant; for I am slow of speech and of a slow tongue . . . Please, Lord, send somebody else." In effect he is saying to the Almighty that He could scarcely have chosen a less qualified spokesman.

And then there is Pharaoh. When the Egyptian monarch is approached with the preposterous request to liberate all this cheap labor, his answer is predictable. What makes the request also grossly offensive is that it is made in the name of some invisible God, as though there were indeed any higher authority than himself, the Pharaoh and Supreme Ruler of the realm. His face was probably as purple as his royal robes and his voice could scarcely conceal his rage as he shot back: "Who is the Lord that *I* should listen to *HIS* voice to let Israel go? I know not the Lord and, moreover, I will not let Israel go."

And then there are the enslaved Israelites. Moses' intercession with Pharaoh on their behalf only enrages the monarch and prompts him to increase their already intolerable burdens. Now they will have to provide their own straw while the quota of bricks remains undiminished. Small wonder then that Moses' promise that the God of their ancestors was about to redeem them from their bondage, left them unmoved and unbelieving. As the Bible tells us (Ex. 6:9), " . . . but they listened not to Moses because of impatience of spirit and cruel bondage."

So here you have the most improbable cast of characters. The self-doubting messenger, the intransigent Pharaoh and the despairing Israelites. And each participant was totally justified in rejecting the assigned role. Moses, Pharaoh and the Israelites were each true to their own selves.

What is more, the plot of the projected drama was as incredulous as it was unprecedented. Never before had a ruler been asked to grant freedom to his slaves who were, after all, his property. Never before had slaves been set free.

Here is where the Divine Playwright enters. He is the true Hero of the Exodus. For it is He who enables a stammering, tongue-tied Moses to be the vehicle for the greatest words ever uttered by a human being. It is He who takes an inflated tyrant and cuts him down to size. It is He who converts an oppressed, down-trodden horde of slaves into "a kingdom of priests and a holy people."

Every year at Pesah time the descendants of those ex-slaves retell and re-enact this ancient drama, thus making it the longest running play in history.

And as we do so we relearn some important truths about the God who wove this implausible story with the most reluctant cast of characters.

He is a God who gives us the courage and the strength to overcome handicaps and adversity, and go on to make something good and beautiful with our flawed human material.

He is the God who humbles the haughty and teaches the tyrant a basic lesson: "Judgment in history," writes the historian Herbert Butterfield, "falls heaviest on those who come to think themselves gods, who fly in the face of Providence, who put their trust in man-made systems and worship the work of their own hands, and who say the strength of their own right arm gave them victory."

He is the God who invests each human being, created in His image, with sanctity and grace, and wants all His children to be free from exploitation, oppression and enslavement.

"Since the days of Moses," wrote Heinrich Heine, "justice speaks with a Hebrew accent." And so does courage, and so does freedom, and so does human dignity.

The Darkness in the Heart

A TEN-YEAR-OLD *yeshivah* student studied for the first time about the plagues that were visited upon the ancient Egyptians.

The ninth plague, he learned, was darkness, a darkness so "thick" that "they saw not one another" (Ex. 10:33).

He asked his rebbe: "What kind of plague was that? After all, they could have lit their lamps and been able to see despite the darkness. Isn't that what they did every night when it got dark?"

The rebbe's smile indicated that he was not displeased by the question. Patting the boy on his head, he said: "The darkness from which the Egyptians suffered was a special kind of darkness. It was not a darkness that affected the eyes; it was a darkness that affected the heart. Physically, they were able to see, but they didn't feel for each other; they didn't care for one another. This is what the Torah means when it says, 'They saw not one another.' They were blind to each other's needs. Each person saw only himself. And that is a terrible plague."

Perhaps the rebbe's answer cannot be harmonized with the literal meaning of the Torah text. But this much is certain, he taught the boy a lesson that goes to the very essence of Judaism.

Much as Judaism is concerned with the relationship between the human being and God, *"beyn adam la-makom,"* it is no less concerned with the relationship between one human being and another, *"beyn adam la-haveyro."*

Judaism expects of us that we shall "see" each person as a human being who has needs, feelings, fears, hungers, hopes just as we do; who is a child of God just as we are; who is fully entitled to be treated with the dignity, justice, and compassion we claim for ourselves.

This message is desperately needed in our time. A popular cartoonist depicted multitudes of ant-sized people at the base of a huge pyramid. The pyramid consisted of four words:

I

ME

MINE

MYSELF

The caption on the cartoon read: "Speaking of American Cults," and it provides a striking illustration of the contemporary plague of darkness—"they saw not one another."

The '70s were labeled the "Me Decade." Have we in the '80s outgrown the narcissistic preoccupation with the self?

A recent study indicates that those over fifty are also joining the "Me Generation." One of America's leading advertising agencies surveyed three separate groups of people—men and women between the ages of 50 and 64, men and women between 65 and 80, and widows between 50 and 64.

Common to all these groups was a feeling that they could indulge themselves fully within the limitations of their income. People who had previously put the needs of their parents, spouses and children above their own are now putting their own needs first. Many were now cashing in their life insurance policies and putting their extra funds into travel, eating out and other personal pleasures. Moreover, the survey found that there was a diminished emphasis on leaving an estate to their children and a greater tendency to spend their own funds now on themselves.

To a certain extent this new development may have some healthy aspects. But carried to extremes, the immersion in the self can have some unfavorable consequences.

A great deal depends upon our ability to "see one another." Our own emotional well-being depends on it. Dr. David Goodman, an authority on mental health, has written, "Mental illness is the price you pay for being absorbed in yourself. Mental health is your reward for devoting yourself to your duties and to the welfare of others."

A rabbi making his way through the corridors of the Albert Einstein Medical Center met a friend who was carrying a heart-breaking burden of family problems, including serious illness and divorce. When he asked her what she was doing in the hospital, she proudly announced that she is a volunteer.

"With all your troubles," he asked, "where do you get the strength to help others?"

"Rabbi," she answered, "this work saves me. If I didn't come here twice a week, I don't think I'd be able to carry on at all."

As he left her, he thought of the answer Dr. Karl Menninger gave when he was asked what to advise a person who felt a nervous breakdown coming on. "I would say to that person: 'Lock up your house, go across the railway tracks, find someone in need and invest yourself in helping that person.'"

The poet put this same basic truth about us in rhyme:

"Man, like the graceful vine, supported lives;
The strength he gains is from the embrace he gives."

The Torah tells us that, during the plague of darkness in Egypt, "all the people Israel had light in all their dwellings." This is the basic challenge that confronts each of us—to keep aglow that light of understanding and caring which enables us to truly see each other. For it is only when we see the humanity in another that we can preserve it within ourselves.

What Keeps the Jew Alive?

A FEW YEARS AGO the syndicated columnist Sydney Harris wrote a piece on the mystery of Jewish survival. Here is how he explained it:

"What has kept the Jewish people alive throughout the centuries has been the awesome paradox of persecution. Left alone to live their lives and practice their beliefs they inevitably tend to dwindle in numbers, to disperse and dilute their ethnic identification.

"Then every so often in history there comes along a devastating persecution that has the very opposite effect of its intention. It militates and mobilizes these people, reminds them of their unique heritage that is regarded as both a blessing and a burden, and re-animates their faith and their sense of identity."

In this reading of Jewish history Sydney Harris is not alone. Many historians have attributed our perseverance to persecution. Thus Lewis Browne, writing during the Hitler era, declared: "We are not so much voluntary Jews as involuntary non-Gentiles . . . Let us be and we will cease to be."

Even our Sages seemed to find in Jewish persecution strong impetus to more intensive Jewish living. They noted that in this *Sidrah* we are told that the Israelites fleeing from Egypt are pursued by Pharaoh who is about to overtake them. The verb form the Torah uses is *"hikriv"* which means "he *brought* near" rather than *"karav,"* "he *came* near," and they deduce from this that the Torah wants us to know that the pursuing Pharaoh *brought* the Israelites nearer to God. In their mortal dread of the avenging tyrant, "they lifted their eyes heavenward, they did penance, and they prayed." Thus Pharaoh's threat accomplished more for the Israelites "than one hundred fasts and prayers."

For all its many advocates, the theory that anti-Semitism keeps Judaism alive is at best a half-truth. The truth is that it is anti-Semitism that threatens Jewish survival. Throughout history it was persecution that decimated Jewish communities, and made escape from Jewishness an attractive alternative. It is anti-Semitism which forever makes the Jew a soliloquizing Hamlet asking: "To be or not to be?" Why remain Jewish in a world where the vicious, the sick, the misinformed repeatedly make it so dangerous to be Jewish?

Why is there no Christian problem of survival? Why is there no Moslem problem of survival? The answer is obvious. It is the persistent efforts to destroy the Jew which create the problem of Jewish survival. Even when it is not actively destroying Jewish lives, anti-Semitism still lurks as a menacing threat, eroding Jewish morale, gnawing away at Jewish security.

If Judaism has survived it is not *because* of anti-Semitism but *despite* it. Anti-Semitism did not strengthen us, it tested our strength. A person who survives a bout of double pneumonia cannot be said to have survived because of the illness. The illness tested his resistance, and his survival demonstrates his ability to triumph over the disease germs that threatened his life.

The Jew survived because he possessed an indestructible will to live. His perennial slogan were the words of the Psalmist: "I shall not die but live and I shall declare the works of the Lord."

A reading of Jewish history will indicate that freedom and toleration need not be inimical to healthy Jewish living. On the contrary, Judaism has enjoyed its most creative periods in periods free from persecution.

The Bible itself is the product of a free people living in its own land, determining its own destiny. That massive product of Jewish genius and intellectual ferment, the Talmud, was created at a time of substantial freedom, and it was only the fear of looming danger that prompted its codification.

Rashi's commentaries, the words of Yehudah Halevi, Ibn Gabirol and almost all the great classics of our heritage were the products of eras when Jews enjoyed freedom and security. The explosion of Jewish spiritual and literary creativity in America and in Israel today provides further overwhelming evidence of Judaism's compatibility with freedom.

To be sure, the freedom to live Judaism also implies the freedom to leave Judaism. That is the price of freedom and we must be prepared to reckon with it. We cannot depend on, much less hope for, anti-Semitism to keep Jews in the fold. A Judaism that was kept alive by its enemies who would not let it die, would scarcely be worth preserving.

Judaism will survive as it always has, proudly and creatively, because its adherents find meaning in their Jewishness, identify with its teachings, find joy in its festivals and holy days, and understand in the depths of their own souls why generations of Jews have resisted every tyranny to remain true to themselves and to their God.

Ours is a tradition ripe with the wisdom of years, strengthened by a thousand anvils. Judaism was a venerable faith before other powerful religions were born. For it, millions were innocently martyred. By it, millions more have nobly and compassionately lived. Despite its antiquity, it evidences none of the infirmities of age. It remains throbbing and dynamic, capable of sustaining its adherents and enriching with its unique genius the larger human family. If we will strive to possess that which is rightfully ours we will enjoy an abundant inheritance past generations have stored up for us to enjoy. And then we will understand why generations of Jews have proclaimed daily in their morning prayers:

> "How fortunate are we!
> How good is our portion!
> How pleasant is our lot!
> How beautiful our heritage!"

The Day that Blesses

WITH THE ANNOUNCEMENT that the *Reader's Digest* has condensed the Bible to sixty percent of its original length, one wit said that he was eager to see which four commandments we don't have to worry about anymore.

In our time we have to worry about all of the Ten Commandments more than ever before. The contemporary moral climate is not too congenial to the observance of these time-hallowed precepts.

Of all the commandments it may be the fourth, "Remember the Sabbath Day to keep it holy," that we have to worry about the most. A nationwide poll rating the commandments in order of significance put the Sabbath Commandment at the very bottom of the list. Would the results have been any different had the poll been conducted exclusively among Jews? I wonder.

In any event, it is worth noting that of all the holy days on the Jewish calendar only the Sabbath was included among the Ten Commandments. None of the Festivals, not even Rosh Hashanah or Yom Kippur, was accorded such an honor. Moreover, the observance of Shabbat is enjoined in the Torah no fewer than twelve times.

Our Sages lavished extraordinary affection upon the Sabbath. They personified it as a beautiful bride, a lovely princess, a gracious queen. Above all, it was a priceless gift from God, a precious link between the paradise that was lost and the paradise that was yet to come.

So deeply did the Sabbath enter into the soul of the Jew and so profound was its influence that Israel Zangwill could speak of it as "the hub of the Jew's universe." Ahad Ha'am saw in it a most potent force for Jewish survival: "One can say without exaggeration that more than the Jew has kept the Sabbath, the Sabbath has kept the Jew." And Abraham Joshua Heschel in his lyrical volume, *The Sabbath*, celebrating the exquisite beauty and magnificent splendor of that holy day, called it a majestic cathedral in time.

If we want to grasp the benevolent influence of the Sabbath we have to see how it impacts on the lives of people. A number of illustrations rush to mind. Henrietta Szold, the founder of Hadassah, would begin her day at 4:30 A.M., end it at midnight, and work busily all the intervening hours. When a close friend once asked her how she was able to work this way, she answered: "There are two reasons: one, I keep the Sabbath; and two, my cast iron stomach." She went on to add that when she lit her candles on Friday she put aside all business and cares and entered into the pure delight of the Sabbath. This day renewed her for the week ahead.

In his book, *This Is My God*, Herman Wouk described how on Friday afternoon he would leave his work on Broadway where he was preparing a play: "Leaving the gloomy theatre, the littered coffee cups, the shouting stagehands, the bedevilled director, I have come home. It has been a startling change, very like a brief return from the wars. My wife and my boys, whose existence I have almost forgotten, are waiting for me, dressed in holiday clothes, and looking to me marvelously attractive . . .

"Saturday is healing for the whole week. The telephone is silent. I can think, read, study, walk, or do nothing. It is an oasis of quiet. When night falls I go back to the wonderful nerve-racking Broadway game. Often I make my best contribution of the week then and there.

"One Saturday night my producer said to me: 'I don't envy you— your religion, but I envy you—your Sabbath.' "

Sam Levenson, the celebrated comedian, once gave us a remarkable insight into what Shabbat meant to the ordinary Jew, the Jew who struggled to eke out a living. Writing of his father, he tells us:

"Now when it came to Papa, he dealt in two times: sacred time and profane time. Making a living, being a sweatshop slave 16 hours a day, this was profane time. But came '*Erev Shabbos*' with the candles lit on the table, and I could see my father change from a sweatshop slave into an angelic figure who had something to do with eternity and sacred time.

"Suddenly the wrinkles came out of his face, and he became again a holy man who was related to the whole universe and to God's destiny for man—which was greater than sitting over a sewing machine in a sweatshop."

Some questions: Do you and I need Shabbat less than Henrietta Szold, Herman Wouk or Sam Levenson's Papa?

In these harried, hurried and harassed times, do we not urgently require some of the spiritual and emotional therapy the Shabbat offers?

At a time when a national magazine designates the computer as "the man of the year" is there not a desperate need to have Shabbat restore our eroded humanity, reaffirm our God-given dignity?

At a time when the integrity of the Jewish family has been seriously undermined, do we not need more than ever before the powerful help of Shabbat to preserve the cohesiveness and promote the togetherness of the family?

At a time when so many worries gnaw at us, so many problems weigh on us, and so many cares feed on us, can we afford to dispense with the joy and the delight the Shabbat can bring us?

The Shabbat, the Torah tells us, is the day that God blessed. It is more. It is the day that blesses those who have the wisdom to observe it.

Judaism will not be saved by any headline-making, breathtaking deeds of valor. It will be sustained by high fidelity to little *mitzvot*.

"Piety," wrote Rabbi Leo Baeck, "especially Jewish piety, respects the little act, the little man, the little matter, the little task, the littly duty. Through the little, religion meets the greatness that lies behind."

The little act, the little task performed regularly and faithfully by little people—this is what gives tone, content and character to a society. We are not called upon to perform extraordinary things. We are asked to perform ordinary things, little things, with extraordinary fidelity.

In her darkness Helen Keller saw a shining truth which can guide each of us. "I long to accomplish a great and noble task, but it is my chief duty and joy to accomplish humble tasks as though they were great and noble . . . For the world is moved along, not only by the mighty shoves of its heroes, but also by the aggregate of tiny pushes of each honest worker."

Let us each contribute our tiny pushes. That's how the world is moved along.

Why "Organized" Religion?

A RABBI WHO TRIED to persuade a gentleman to join his congregation was told by the man, "I appreciate the importance of religion, but I don't believe in *organized* religion." To which the rabbi replied, "You'll love our synagogue. It's completely disorganized."

I do not know whether the solicited gentleman joined the "disorganized" synagogue. But he expressed a frequently heard opinion. We have all heard people label "religion" good and "organized religion" as either bad or quite expendable.

These same people would not say, "I believe in medicine but I do not believe in medical schools, hospitals and clinics."

Nor would they say, "I believe in law and justice but I do not believe in law schools, courts and police."

Nor, "I love art and beauty but I do not believe in art schools and museums."

If medicine, justice and art are worth fostering, there must be institutions devoted to those purposes. And so it is with religion.

This realization came to us early in Jewish history. In this Torah portion we read that shortly after our ancestors left Egypt, they were commanded: "Let them build Me a sanctuary so that I may dwell among them" (Ex. 25:8). This injunction was the first effort to "organize" religion, and for more than 3,000 years, in good times and bad, in lands of freedom and oppression, our people were builders of sanctuaries.

[TERUMAH]   67

What purpose do our sanctuaries, or "organized" synagogues, serve?

Let us list briefly some of the major contributions the synagogue makes to the tone and texture of Jewish life.

The synagogue provides the ideal Jewish setting for worship, where that which is noblest within ourselves reaches out toward that which is highest in the universe—God.

In a noisy world, it enables us to pause periodically to listen to the still small voice of the spirit.

The synagogue provides a place of assembly for the Jewish community and for the many organizations of Jewish youth and adults. It is the recognized address of the Jewish community for Jew and non-Jew alike.

The synagogue is the institution that best preserves the Jewish heritage and most effectively transmits the teachings of the prophets, the wisdom of our Sages and teachers.

The synagogue has been the most potent force for Jewish continuity throughout the vicissitudes of our history. It continues to nourish the Jewish will to survive and to provide joy in living as a Jew.

The synagogue raises to loftiest significance the great milestones from birth to death by clothing them in the warmth of hallowed words and sacred rituals, and by providing a community with which to share these exalted occasions.

The synagogue keeps alive and articulates our people's most treasured memories, our most fervent beliefs and our most cherished hopes.

The synagogue provides a fellowship for Jews who take their heritage seriously and who look to it to provide guidance, solace and inspiration.

The synagogue nurtures our faith in the coming of an era of peace and justice for all people; it gives us the courage to work for God's kingdom and the patience to hopefully wait for it.

The synagogue drapes each human being with highest dignity, confers upon life ultimate meaning, invests the universe with high purpose and sees in Jewish destiny cosmic significance.

The synagogue richly merits the tribute paid to it by Robert T. Herford, a Christian scholar: "In all their long history, the Jewish people have done scarcely anything more wonderful than to create the synagogue. No human institution has a longer continuous history, and none has done more for the uplifting of the human race."

However great was the role of the synagogue in elevating the human race, its role in giving meaning and substance to Jewish life was even greater.

In his autobiography, *Dreamer's Journey Home*, Morris Raphael Cohen makes the following confession:

"In my youth I would not have mentioned this for I then joined in the romantic and uncritical disparagement of all priesthoods to extol the revolutionary or reforming prophets. But as I grew older I began to recognize that while the inspiration of the prophets is necessary, men cannot live on revolutions alone. The preaching of prophets would be merely an emotional indulgence if it did not find embodiment in some law, custom or ritual to make smooth and channelize our daily life."

We might add that the preaching of the prophets also needs embodiment in an institution, and for us that institution is the synagogue.

The synagogue is the central institution which both symbolizes Jewish continuity and which made that continuity possible. When we join a synagogue, we join the mighty company of Jews throughout the ages who took seriously the divine command spoken to our ancestors just as soon as they left Egypt: "Let them build Me a sanctuary so that I may dwell among them."

The Internal Light

SOME ELEMENTARY school children visited our synagogue as part of their social studies project. I explained to them the significance of the various synagogue symbols including the *Ner Tamid*, the eternal light which burns constantly above the Holy Ark.

I pointed out that we use the eternal light because of the verse in the Torah (Ex. 27:20): "And you shall command the people of Israel that they bring pure olive oil beaten for the light to cause a lamp to burn continually . . . ."

Shortly after the visit I received a package of thank you letters from the youngsters. The letter I remember best was from a 5th-grader who wrote in part: "I especially liked your explanation of the *internal* light."

The youngster had stumbled on a profound truth about us. We do indeed each possess an internal light and that may very well be the most important human endowment we receive at birth. It is a spark of divinity kindled within each of us.

The "internal light" has been variously identified. One writer described it as "the soft whispers of God in man." George Washington admonished: "Labor hard to keep alive in your breast that little spark of celestial fire called conscience." Lord Byron put his perception of the "internal light" into poetry:

> "Whatever creed be taught or land be trod,
> Man's conscience is the oracle of God."

Our Bible described the "internal light" in these words: "The spirit of man is God's candle." It is this built-in candle which is our most distinctive quality. It is this light which enables us to distinguish between good and evil, right and wrong, compassion and cruelty, truth and falsehood. It is this unique capacity which sets us apart from the rest of the animal kingdom.

Thus Maimonides observed in his *Commentary on the Mishnah*: "What restrains beasts from doing harm is external—a bridle or a bit, but man's restraints lie within himself."

The "internal light" does more than equip us with the ability to make moral distinctions and decisions. It also confers upon each of us supreme value. We are each special and unique. We are each a sacred refraction of divinity. God has shared with every one of us a measure of His illumination.

When we forget our inherent God-given worth, we look to others for applause, for approval, for validation. We become like street beggars with our little tin cups extended soliciting a few coins of praise. We permit others to determine whether and how much we matter.

Lloyd C. Douglas pointed to this truth: "The greatest thing anybody can do is to build himself up strongly on the inside. The trouble with most people is that they don't think enough of the value of their own inner selves."

How much we value our own inner selves is a crucial dimension of our personalities. It affects every aspect of our behavior. Our ability to learn and grow, our choice of careers, companions and mates, our likelihood of succeeding in our chosen vocation—all are intimately related to the degree of our self-esteem.

One of the most nourishing ways to enhance our self-esteem is to remind ourselves that we are each the bearers of God's candle. To be human is to be distinguished, to possess infinite worth.

A recent illustration in the newspaper showed a small boy with big wistful eyes, his hair flopping over his forehead. He is surrounded by these words: "I know I'm Somebody Cause God Don't Make No Junk."

What the caption lacks in grammar it compensates in insight.

Our "internal light" not only affirms our God-given worth, it also enables us to determine what Claude Bernard, a famous chemist, called our "internal environment."

It may be dark and gloomy on the outside, but within we can keep aglow the candle of faith. There may be a penetrating chill of despair in the air, but we can keep burning the candle of hope. We may not be able to do anything about the weather outside, but our finger is on the internal thermostat. The Torah tells us that when the plague of darkness descended upon the Egyptians "for all the children of Israel there was light in their dwellings."

Abraham Lincoln, whose birthday falls at this time of the year, was profoundly aware of the importance of keeping aglow the "internal light." "I desire," he wrote, "so to conduct the affairs of this administration that if at the end, when I come to lay down the reins of power, I have lost every other friend on earth, I shall at least have one friend left, and that friend will be deep inside me."

And one thing more our "internal light" does for us. It illumines for us the path that leads to creativity and self-expression.

A Parisian artist once complained to the renowned sculptor Jacques Lipchitz that he was unhappy with the quality of the light he was painting. He had even gone to Morocco in search of a change of light but to no avail. "An artist's light," Lipchitz told him, "comes not from without, but from within."

And so it is with all of us.

The Obsolete Commandment

TWO YOUNG MEN were leaving a service during which they had heard a sermon on the Ten Commandments. After a few moments of silence one of them muttered: "Well, at least I never made any graven images."

The second commandment does seem to be so universally observed that it has been called "the obsolete commandment." Who worships graven images today, anyway?

When we read in this *Sidrah* that our ancestors fashioned a golden calf and worshipped it, it all sounds so very primitive. We're way beyond that, aren't we? Josephus was so embarrassed by the golden calf episode that he omitted it altogether from his Greek narrative of Jewish "Antiquities." Why tell the "goyim" about this spiritual relapse our ancestors suffered only forty days after they stood at Mount Sinai?

On second thought, however, perhaps the worship of the golden calf is not merely an incident that happened long ago; it may even be a metaphor depicting our own situation.

A magazine cartoon showed two cigar-smoking, well-dressed men relaxing in huge upholstered chairs. One confides to the other: "It was terrible! I dreamed the dollar was no longer worth worshipping!"

"Contemporary life," wrote Will Herberg, "is idolatry ridden to an appalling degree." Perhaps the second commandment isn't obsolete after all.

Somebody has identified a new disease in our country. It is called "Materio-Sclerosis," an insatiable hunger for the acquisition of things, more things, more expensive things.

On any given Sunday morning our pulpits and airwaves carry messages denouncing communism as "godless materialism" or "atheistic materialism." How about our own brand of materialism?

The Communists admit they are materialistic but we deny it. We imprint on all our currency (in very small letters) "In God We Trust." But do we trust in God as much as we trust in that money? Did Dr. George A. Butterick exaggerate when he said that in our society success consists of "a fairly nasty mixture of cash and gadgets?"

The officiating clergyman at the funeral of Harold Wallace Ross, the editor and founder of *The New Yorker*, said of him: "He hated all tyrannies, not least the insidious tyranny of things." In this land of the free many of us have succumbed to the tyranny of things. We suffer from materio-sclerosis. In the inner shrine of our personal sanctuaries, there stands a calf of gold.

All this is not to say that we are supposed to renounce all striving for wealth and take to the hills. Judaism never considered poverty a virtue. As one of Sholom Aleichem's characters says: "Poverty is no crime but it is no great honor either."

Judaism was profoundly concerned with the deep wounds that poverty inflicts on the soul no less than on the body. At a time of massive unemployment in our land, our tradition bids us to address ourselves with all our might to the solution of this terrible problem, to give it top priority on our collective agenda.

Just as Judaism did not consider poverty a virtue, it did not consider wealth a sin. It did not say with the New Testament that "It is easier for a camel to pass through the eye of a needle than it is for a rich man to enter into the kingdom of Heaven."

What Judaism did do was to alert us to the perils inherent in possessions, the tyranny which lurks in things, the danger of becoming afflicted with materio-sclerosis and worshipping the golden calf.

What are some of the symptoms of this idolatry? We make a graven image of gold when we sacrifice our health for it, when we surrender our moral integrity for it, when we neglect our families for it, when we betray our principles for it.

We worship the golden calf when we forget that some of the most precious things in life cannot be bought with gold. Genuine love, true friendship, a clear conscience, strength of character, peace of mind, serenity of spirit, self-respect—these are not listed on any exchange.

Henrik Ibsen spoke directly on this theme when he wrote: "Money can buy the husk of things but not the kernel. It brings you food but not appetite, medicine but not health, acquaintances but not friends, servants but not faithfulness, days of joy but not peace or happiness."

Before we leave our theme we ought to note that the Torah tells us that our ancestors used their treasures not only to fashion a golden calf but also to build a sanctuary in the desert. This prompted a rabbinic comment: "With jewels they sinned and with jewels they were restored to God's favor."

Gold need not become an object of worship. Used with wisdom and compassion it can help bring an awareness of God's presence even in a wilderness.

Use and Misuse

~~※~~

A CRITIC once wrote of a volume under review: "The cruelest thing you could do to this book is to read it a second time." One of the hallmarks of our Bible which makes it a classic is its capacity to yield new meanings and fresh insights every time we read it.

A case in point is this *Sidrah*. Truth to tell it is hardly a candidate for anyone's favorite Torah portion. It consists largely of a listing of the materials that went into the construction of the tabernacle in the wilderness, and the dimensions of each of its important appurtenances. Those of us who do not have any conspicuous architectural skills or curiosity, will probably skim over most of these chapters in a hurry.

But a rabbinic comment on this *Sidrah* calls attention to a truth worth pondering. Our Sages pointed out that in the previous Torah portion we read that our ancestors used their jewels to fashion a gold calf around which they danced as they chanted the idolatrous heresy: "This is your God, O Israel, who brought you out of the land of Egypt" (Ex. 32:4). In *this* Torah portion we read that these same ancestors used their jewels to build a tabernacle to the glory of the one God.

This use of the same materials for such vastly divergent purposes prompted our Sages to comment: "With earrings they sinned and with earrings they were restored to God's favor."

In this brief comment the rabbis emphasized the ambivalent

character of our possessions. They can be used for the meanest or the noblest purposes. They are in themselves morally neutral. Whether they are good or bad depends upon us, on how we use them.

This simple truth has wider ramifications. It applies to other crucial areas of our lives. Science which has done so much to prolong human life and improve its quality was used by the Nazis to build more efficient gas chambers and to conduct the most brutal experiments without anesthesia on men and women. The automobile which rushes a physician on a mission of mercy, carries a drunken driver on a mission of murder.

An article on lasers in one of our national magazines points out that next to the computer they are the most versatile invention of the twentieth century. Lasers are still in the nursery stage but the infant is growing fast. Lasers are already cutting concrete and steel and are being used to perform delicate eye surgery. Lasers may turn out to be an unprecedented boon by generating a new and inexhaustible source of energy or they may further imperil our fragile planet by leading to ever more destructive and devastating weaponry.

The road to hell is paved with good inventions.

What is true of our possessions, of science, and indeed of all the instruments we use is also true of most of our human endowments and emotions.

A *Hasid* once asked his *Rebbe* why the Almighty created the quality of human skepticism. After all, he said, everything that the Holy One, blessed be He, made, He fashioned for some benevolent purpose. But what possible benefit can skepticism bring? It only leads people to doubt the existence of the Almighty Himself.

To which the *Rebbe* replied: "My son, skepticism does indeed serve on occasion a most noble purpose. When a poor man comes to you for help do not send him away with the assurance that God will help him. At that time you must be a skeptic and doubt that God will help him. You must help him yourself."

Is anger good or bad. Again, it depends. To be sure anger is only one letter removed from danger. It wrecks homes, destroys friendships and frequently leads to impulsive violence. But on the other hand, as Tevya would say, the prophets were God's angry men. Oppression made them angry, injustice made them angry, human cruelty and dishonesty made them angry. And if they are still revered today it is due in no small measure to their marvelous capacity to get angry at the right time to the right degree, for the right reasons.

What is true of our instruments and our human endowments is also true of our circumstances. They too are neutral. Whether they bless us or break us depends on how we confront them, how we use them.

Edmund Ward in *The Main Chance* advises: "Drink champagne for defeats as well as victories. It tastes the same, and you need it more." I'll drink to that! But for a different reason. We should drink champagne to defeats because no defeat is final and no defeat cannot be used to teach us an important lesson.

William Bolitho has illumined this truth for us: "The most important thing in life," he wrote, "is not simply to capitalize on your gains. Any fool can do that. The important thing is to profit from your losses. That requires intelligence and it marks the difference between a man of sense and a fool.

In 1849 Nathaniel Hawthorne was dismissed from his government job in the customhouse. He came home a beaten man.

His wife listened to him as he poured out his heart, threw a few logs on the fire, set pen, ink and paper on the table, put her arms around him and said: "Now you will be able to write your novel." He did. That's how *The Scarlet Letter* came to be written.

In 1845, Heinrich Graetz, a newly ordained rabbi, applied for an important synagogue pulpit in Upper Silesia. During his trial sermon he developed pulpit palpitations, lost his train of thought and stammered through an incoherent sermon. He did not get the pulpit. His disappointment was crushing. Happily for us he went on to discover his great literary and scholarship powers and he became the eminent historian whose six volumes of Jewish history remain classics in their field.

A friend who was showing some slides of his pilgrimage to Israel projected one picture which baffled him. He paused a while and then confessed: "I'm not sure whether this is a picture of a sunrise or a sunset."

Unwittingly, he made a profound statement about many of life's experiences. So often we think we are going through a "sunset" and night is approaching and the outlook is black. But we later discover to our delight that it wasn't a "sunset" after all. It was really a "sunrise" ushering in a new day with new beginnings, new possibilities and new hope.

How to Measure a Person

IN HIS AUTOBIOGRAPHY entitled *Wayward Child,* Addison Gayle Jr. recalls a childhood incident that left an enduring mark. The time was the '40s and the place was Newport News, Virginia.

A young black boy is told by his father that he is running for Congress. The lad asks his father whether he expects to win.

"What kind of a question is that?" his father replies. "Of course I won't win. Those pecks would never let a black man win."

"Why you running, then?"

"So that some day *you* can win."

That day young Addison learned an important lesson. High aspiration has its own rewards even though the results are not immediately apparent.

This truth is vividly illustrated in this week's prophetic reading.

When King Solomon dedicates the magnificent Temple he built in Jerusalem, he recalls that his father, King David, had wanted "to build a house for the Lord, the God of Israel," but he was denied the privilege. That very desire, however, was found praiseworthy by God. " . . . You did well that it was in your heart." God further assures him that his son "shall build the house for My name" (I Kings 8:17–19).

The aspiration of the father became the achievement of the son. Moreover, the father himself became a better human being for the high goal that he had pursued. "You did well that it was in your heart."

So much of life compels us to occupy ourselves with our small daily needs and concerns. There are mundane chores to be done, assignments to be met, routine duties to be carried out. In addition there is the perpetual demand to make ends meet. All of these pedestrian concerns tend to lower our sights, to narrow the range of our vision. In our preoccupation with immediates we tend to lose sight of ultimates.

The *Plodder's Petition* echoes a prayer we might each offer from time to time:

> "Lord let me not be too content
> With life in trifling service spent.
> Make me aspire!
> When days with petty cares are filled,
> Let me with fleeting thoughts be thrilled,
> Of something higher."

> (Helen Gilbert)

Our genuine need for thoughts of "something higher" is something we all feel in our finer moments. "A map of the world," wrote Oscar Wilde, "that does not include Utopia, is not worth glancing at." We need long-range goals to keep from being frustrated by short-range failures. We need our Utopias to keep life from becoming coarsened. When Emerson urged: "Hitch your wagon to a star," he knew that wagons cannot reach stars, but the very effort might keep the wagon from getting mired in the gutter.

A good measure of a human being is not in what he achieves as much as in what he strives to achieve. A man can be measured by the size of his goals. He who aims high and fails is in many ways a taller person than he who aims low and succeeds.

It is no small consolation to earn the divine verdict: "You did well that it was in your heart."

The First Lesson

OF THE FIVE BOOKS of the Torah, Leviticus, which we read at this time of the year, is the most difficult and the least interesting for the modern reader. It is largely concerned with the details of the ancient institution of animal sacrifice which came to an abrupt end when the second Temple in Jerusalem was destroyed almost two thousand years ago.

And yet for all its lack of appeal or drama it was with Leviticus that Jewish children in olden days would begin their study of the Torah. Not the absorbing stories of Genesis, nor the exciting events in Exodus, but the dry, uninspiring laws concerning sacrifices constituted their introduction to sacred Scripture. Why?

Our Sages in the Midrash gave a charming answer to this question: "Little children are pure and the sacrifices are pure; so let those who are pure come and occupy themselves with things that are pure."

There may be another reason why Jewish youngsters began their Torah studies with Leviticus. Perhaps our teachers wanted to impress upon the young minds at their earliest opportunity the inescapable truth that sacrifice is at the very center of life. Nothing worthwhile in life is ever achieved without it.

Moreover—and this might have been the most important reason—unless they learned the meaning of sacrifice in their own lives, they would never make very much of themselves.

This is a lesson worth pondering in an age dedicated to instant self-gratification, self-indulgence and self-pampering. If we want the rewards of achievement we have to be ready to pay the awesome price achievement sternly demands.

One of the popular illusions of our time views life as a giant commissary from which we are entitled to draw unlimited rations of food and clothing, power and privilege. That is a caricature of life. Life, the Torah would remind us, is an altar, and the things that go on an altar are sacrifices. Until we have learned that basic truth we are not yet ready for mature and meaningful living.

When Isaac Stern concluded a concert recital one evening, he was approached by an ardent admirer who exclaimed rapturously: "Oh Mr. Stern, I would give anything to be able to play the violin as magnificently as you do!" To which the maestro replied softly: "Would you give twelve hours a day?"

Genius has been defined as one percent inspiration and ninety-nine percent perspiration. This comment prompted my favorite cartoon friend Ziggy to boast: "I am ninety-nine percent genius."

Perhaps the percentages are not all that one-sided, but who will deny that genius is indeed the capacity for taking infinite pains, the capacity for doing without today so that you can do with tomorrow, the ability to make demands of ourselves before we are entitled to expect anything from others.

A successful artist in a recent interview said that in order to be a good artist a person "must be willing to be ruthless with himself." Robert Frost was pointing in the same direction when he spoke of the "pain" of poetry: "Poetry, like all birth and creativity, is accompanied by pain and sacrifice."

Great character, great homes, great lives—all are built on sacrifice. And so is a vital, rewarding Jewish life.

"No religion is worth its salt," wrote Rabbi Abba Hillel Silver, "which does not make great demands upon its adherents. . . . Too many of our people want an easy-going religion, one which does not interfere with their leisure, their sleep, or their television, which calls for no study and no observance, which does not challenge or disturb them, a religion without any spiritual travail, without any stab of thought or conscience, without any sacrifices, the religion of a self-pampering people. No religion has ever survived in that kind of an emotional and intellectual vacuum. Judaism least of all."

Perhaps the time has come to go back to the first lesson.

Our Enduring Hope

THIS *SIDRAH* contains the unspectacular and unexceptional verse: "You shall eat no manner of blood" (Lev. 7:26). With minor variations this injunction against eating blood occurs in four other passages in the Torah.

Well, if the verse is "unspectacular and unexceptional," why call attention to it? The answer is to be found in history, which wrote a bloody commentary of this verse.

One of the most pernicious slanders against the Jewish people was the so-called "ritual murder" charge. According to this vicious myth, Jews murdered Christians, especially Christian children, and used the blood of their victims for such ritual purposes as baking Matzot for Passover.

Ironically, this charge leveled by Christians against Jews was first made against the early Christians by the Greeks and Romans. Thus we find the Christian writer Tertullian, pleading with the Romans to give no credence to the blood libel. "For we [Christians] do not include even animals' blood in our natural diet."

This calumny was first hurled against the Jews in Norwich, England, in 1144, and then it appeared with distressing frequency in every century and in almost every country in Europe. Thus, one historian writes: "The blood-libel strutted its ghoulish antics before the footlights of history, attired in the latest fashion, adapting itself to contemporary situations, tastes and emphases in each century."

Almost invariably, the cost in Jewish life was heavy. In 1290, the ritual murder libel resulted in the expulsion of all Jews from England.

In 1840 the notorious Damascus Affair took place in Syria where the disappearance of a Christian monk was blamed on the Jews of that city. This, despite the fact that it was known that he had quarreled violently with a Mohammedan. A number of Jews were arrested and "confessions" were extracted by torture from several of them. Some died during the torture. To aggravate matters, the consul of France involved himself in the affair by supporting the monks. Ultimately the Jews were exonerated but not before some foreign governments, including the United States, had intervened in the matter.

The most stunning revival of this myth in the twentieth century took place in Russia, in the famous Mendel Beilis trial in 1913, that attracted worldwide attention.

In September 1911, the body of a murdered child was found in Kiev, near a brickyard run by a Jew named Mendel Beilis. Although it was clear that the child had been killed by a gang of thieves to which the child's mother belonged, Beilis was brought to trial on the charge of ritual murder. The Czarist minister of justice made every effort to pin the charge on Beilis, but even his handpicked judge and jury were unable to find Beilis guilty. The outbreak of World War I put an end to the proceedings.

Not surprisingly, the Nazis broadcast this infamous lie in their many propaganda organs and various Arab publications and media have also attempted to arouse anti-Jewish sentiment by repeating the ritual blood libel.

In 1972, the Egyptian daily Al Akhbar informed its readers: "The Jews have what is called the great feast of Passover, or the feast of unleavened bread, which is conducted amid the letting of blood from a non-Jew. Following that, they take part of the flesh of the man and mix it with the Matzah. The slaughter is done by the rabbi himself. . . . This is our enemy and this is his character."

One more historical footnote. In 1475 in the city of Trent, a 2-year-old boy, Simon, was found dead by one of the 25 Jews of the city. A "trial" of virtually all the Jews was carried out and at least 12 Jews were executed. In 1965, almost five centuries later, the Vatican exonerated the victims of what it called "a judicial assassination."

So frequently did this calumny of the blood libel reappear that some Jewish authorities advised against the use of red wine at the Seder for fear that its color might arouse the suspicions of the non-Jewish community.

Jewish tradition requires that all blood be drained from meat before it may be eaten. If a single drop of blood is found on the yolk of an egg, the egg may not be eaten.

Judaism took seriously the injunction: "You shall eat no manner of blood." Is it too much to hope that one day all people will consider human blood too precious to be shed?

On Keeping Kosher

IN A BIOGRAPHY of the late Dr. Stephen Wise, there is a fascinating incident which provides a telling commentary on the powerful role that the laws of *Kashrut* have played in our history from the time they were promulgated in the Torah down to modern times.

When the American Standard Bible Committee, a Protestant group, was preparing to work on a new translation of the Hebrew Bible, the committee invited the well-known Jewish Biblical scholar, Dr. Harry Orlinsky, to join in the endeavor. For a variety of reasons, Dr. Orlinsky was reluctant to do so. When the invitation was repeated, Dr. Orlinsky, who was then a member of the faculty of the Jewish Institute of Religion, decided to ask its president, Dr. Stephen Wise, for his advice.

Dr. Wise urged Dr. Orlinsky to accept the invitation but to remember that he was going to serve on that committee as the representative of the Jewish people. Therefore, Dr. Orlinsky was not to work with the committee on the Sabbath nor was he to partake of *trefah* food in the company of his Christian colleagues.

What is so striking about this conversation is the fact that Stephen Wise himself, as a leader of Reform Judaism, was not especially observant of the traditional laws relating to Shabbat or *Kashrut*. But he understood how crucial Shabbat and *Kashrut* observance had always been in Jewish life and he wanted Dr. Orlinsky to honor these sancta when he worked with Christians as a representative of the Jewish people.

As a student of Jewish history, Dr. Wise knew well how often Jews made great sacrifices to observe *Kashrut*. One of the first recorded Jewish martyrs was the aged scribe Eliezer. When the Greeks at the time of the Maccabees attempted to compel him to eat pig's flesh, he permitted himself to be killed rather than transgress the laws of the Torah.

The historian Josephus tells of the Essenes, who during the war against the Romans though "racked and twisted, burnt and broken, and made to pass through every instrument of torture in order to induce them to blaspheme their lawgiver or to eat some forbidden thing, refused to yield to either demand, nor even once did they cringe to their persecutors or shed a tear."

And so it went down the centuries. During the Inquisition many Marranos in Spain risked their lives to obtain Kosher meat. This was considered an act of heresy and could be punished by death.

At the time of the Crusades even forced conversions could not separate many Jews from their observance of the Dietary Laws. Thus a contemporary chronicler wrote: "It is fitting that I should recount their praise, for whatever they ate . . . they did at the peril of their lives. They would ritually slaughter animals for food according to the Jewish tradition."

Countless incidents of fidelity to the Dietary Laws at great personal peril are also part of the spiritual legacy of the black night in the Nazi kingdom of evil.

The Talmud tells us that those *Mitzvot* for which our people risked their very lives became especially dear to them. Who will deny that the Mitzvah of *Kashrut* is most prominent among them?

Modern times have not dealt kindly with the Dietary Laws. They are derided as constituting a religion of "pot-and-pan-theism." Originally, it is claimed, they were a valuable safeguard to health, but today government agencies assure the quality of the food we eat. The truth is that in urging upon us the observance of *Kashrut*, the Torah links it not to healthiness but to holiness.

Further, it is argued, the Dietary Laws prevent social and political integration. Their observance is an unnecessary burden. And besides, it is expensive to keep them.

But if I read the signs correctly, *Kashrut* is making a comeback. It's becoming quite kosher to keep Kosher.

Before each of the Jewish holidays, American newspapers pass along to their readers Kosher recipes for traditional holiday foods.

Stockholders of major corporations are given the option of selecting a Kosher lunch at the annual meeting. All airlines and many ships offer Kosher meals, as do many non-Jewish hospitals.

It is almost routine today for the White House to serve a Kosher meal whenever the function is in honor of an Israeli dignitary.

Kashrut has also become more widely practiced among Reform rabbis. Today it is no longer unusual to meet a Reform rabbi whose home is Kosher.

A celebrated sociologist once observed that what the children of immigrants wish to forget, the grandchildren wish to remember. In many instances this is proving true as it relates to *Kashrut*. Why do the grandchildren reclaim the discarded practices? Let one of the grandchildren give the answer.

In *Sh'ma*, a fine biweekly magazine, Andy and Marian Bowman wrote a piece entitled: "... And So We Became Kosher." She is a former special education teacher "now raising a family," and he is the Chief Federal Public Defender for the State of Connecticut. Here is what they wrote in part:

"It's a wonderful feeling to know that any Jew can come to our home and eat with us without feeling uncomfortable. It's also wonderful to feel that we have undertaken a discipline in our home which is peculiarly Jewish in nature, for we believe that *Kashrut* is an act of faith.

"... to us the extra attention that we pay to eating in our Kosher home gives us a feeling of warmth and closeness to a heritage we take pride in and to a people to whose survival we are dedicated. It is our way of expressing who and what we are in a basic, personal and positive way."

A Drop in a Bucket

THE OBSTETRICIAN was not at home. His five-year-old daughter answered the doorbell. "Is your daddy in?" asked an excited stranger. "No, he's gone," the little girl replied. "When will he return?" "I don't know. He's out on an eternity case."

The little girl was right. Every child is an eternity case—the heir of all that has gone before, the molder of all that is to be.

The birth of a child is such a commonplace thing. It happens 200,000 times a day. And yet each child is an original, altogether unique and so enormously special. Each child is a miracle, a tiny bundle of infinite possibilities, mysterious and unpredictable.

At the beginning of this *Sidrah*, we read a simple awesome passage: "If a woman shall bear a child . . . " (Lev. 12:2). Do we know what secret that child carries, what hidden splendor that tiny frame embodies?

In a world where there are more than four billion of us crowding in a shrinking globe and where so much justified concern is being devoted to the prevention of the uncontrolled multiplication of the human species, it is difficult to preserve a sense of awe and wonder and mystery in the presence of the individual human being.

In a world where machines can outperform us to a distressing degree, it is not easy to maintain a sense of reverence for the human personality. A computer in England trying to determine the respective odds on the player and the banker in a card game called baccarat, took 45 minutes to complete the calculations involving more than one billion separate operations. An Einstein could not have done this task alone if he lived to be 1000 years old.

In a world where people tend more and more to be reduced to statistical data, efficiency is frequently purchased at the cost of our humanity.

With all these dehumanizing influences at work in our times it is all the more vital that we recall the teaching of our tradition which underscores the uniqueness of each of us.

Our Sages dramatize this point in a vivid parable. A mortal king, they said, when he wishes to make many coins, creates one mold and with that mold he stamps out all the coins he needs. Each coin is exactly like every other coin. God, however, created all men from but one mold, and yet no two individuals are exactly alike.

Judaism reminds us that there is no common man. Each one of us is uncommon. There has been nothing like us ever, nor will there ever be. There is no such thing as an average man except on the graphs and the charts of the statisticians.

"Every single man is a new thing in the world and is called upon to fulfill his particularity in the world." Thus taught the *Hasidic Rebbe*, Yechiel Michael of Zlotchov.

In each of us all the past centuries coalesce. In each of us all the future centuries have their beginnings. In each of us there are found very special endowments. "It is a pleasant fact," said Henry Thoreau, "that you will know no man long, however low in the social scale, however poor, miserable, intemperate and worthless he may appear to be, a mere burden to society, but you will find at last that there is something which he understands and can do better than any other."

In the eyes of our Creator we are not statistics. We are each the object of God's care and compassion. We are each counted. We are each remembered. We are each one—one unique man, one special woman, one precious little child.

And we each have extraordinary capacities and all kinds of latent force. We each have the power to transform our lives. We can each make a decisive difference in the world.

One of the most debilitating questions is the one which is so frequently asked rhetorically, with a despairing shrug of the shoulders. What can one person do? What can I do to affect the moral fiber of a community? Go fight City Hall! What can I do about raising the level of jungle ethics that prevails in the business world? You have to play their game. What can I do about the symptoms of the deterioration of Judaism in America? There are great factors at work beyond my control. I am just a drop in the bucket.

Well, one man who has made a decisive difference in the spiritual texture and moral tone of our time, Albert Schweitzer, has something very different to say about the human "drop in the bucket." "We see no power in a drop of water; but let it get into a crack in the rock and be turned to ice and it splits the rock; turned into steam, it drives the pistons of the most powerful engines."

We each possess enormous potential power and energy within ourselves. If we utilize that power we can indeed effect decisive changes within ourselves. We can leave the world a little better and a little cleaner than we found it.

Words Are Holy

THE PUN HAS BEEN denigrated as the lowest form of humor—when someone else thinks of it first. Puns are usually short quips followed by long groans. But Louis Untermeyer was quite on target when he said that punning is like poetry—something everyone belittles and everyone attempts. And I believe that the pun is often mightier than the sword.

A sharp case in point is the title of this *Sidrah*. It is *Metzora* which means "leper." But our ancient Rabbis, who often used the lowly pun to teach an exalted truth, read that Hebrew word as two Hebrew words—*Motzi ra,* "He who spreads evil." They then proceeded to denounce the sin of spreading evil, the sin of slander and malicious gossip, as a loathsome moral disease, a disease to be as strenuously avoided as leprosy.

Thus they taught that *leshon ha-ra*, evil speech, spoken of a third person, kills three people: the one who speaks it, the one who accepts it and the one of whom it is spoken.

Another Sage declared that he who spreads an evil report against another is as guilty as though he had violated all the teachings of the five books of the Torah.

The confessional on Yom Kippur lists forty-four sins for which we ask to be forgiven. Of these no fewer than ten are sins of speech.

The terrible thing about the malicious word is that it is so irretrievable. An old Jewish story tells of a woman who came to her rabbi on a wintry day with a terrible sense of guilt. She had spread a very unkind story about another woman in the town, and had just learned that the story had no basis whatever in fact. What should she do?

The rabbi told her that she would have to do two things. First, she would have to take the feathers from one of her pillows and place one feather on the doorstep of each of the houses in the little town. After she completed this task she should return and the rabbi would give her a second task. The woman left and returned the following day. "What shall I do now?" she asked. "Now," said the rabbi, "go gather up all the feathers from each of the houses where you put them."

"But rabbi," protested the woman, "that is impossible. The wind has already scattered them far and wide." "Indeed, it has," said the rabbi. "To gather up those feathers is as impossible as to take back the harsh words you spoke. You would do well to remember that before you speak in the future."

The tongue is in a very wet place and it is so easy for it to slip. And how often do we inflict with our tongue the kind of blows which burn deeper and hurt so much longer than any physical blows we can inflict.

Dr. Paul Tournier, the Swiss psychiatrist, tells of a woman he treated. She was experiencing a distressing sense of unworthiness and emptiness in her life. After a period of counseling the patient recalled a telling incident from her childhood. She had been in another room and overheard her mother say to her father about her: "We could have done without that one." That careless remark had twisted a life out of shape.

A similar story appeared in one of the advice columns in the newspaper. When the letter writer was five years old he was playing in the kitchen with his three-year-old brother Joe. In the course of their innocent play the younger boy fell against the hot stove and burned his face. The burn left a bad scar.

From that day on, every time people asked about the cause of the scar, his mother would say, "His brother burned him." The letter writer continues: "This went on for many years. Each time my mother said, 'His brother burned him,' I wanted to die. Never once did she suggest it was an accident.

"I'm a grown man now, but the burden of looking at Joe and knowing I was the cause of his scar still bothers me. How simple it would have been if mother had worded it differently."

Many of us who wouldn't dream of lifting a hand against another human being think nothing of inflicting damaging blows with our tongues. When we were kids there was a popular ditty which we used to defend ourselves against verbal onslaughts:

"Sticks and stones will break my bones
But names will never harm me."

We don't believe that anymore. Nor do we believe one of the cynical slogans of our time, "words are cheap."

A bride and groom under the canopy, betting their lives on each other and summing up this fateful decision in a few words, do not believe that words are cheap.

A young man being interviewed by a prospective employer for a position for which he has prepared himself over long, hard years, does not believe that words are cheap.

A lawyer pleading desperately for the life of his client does not believe that words are cheap.

Children gathered around the bedside of a dying father, who is leaving his last verbal legacy, do not believe that words are cheap.

At such moments surely words become freighted with an urgency and a decisiveness which leave their permanent imprint upon human lives. At such critical junctures we accept the judgment of our tradition that "Life and death are in the power of the tongue."

But Judaism goes beyond these spectacular and dramatic moments. It tells us that at all times, in every circumstance, words are holy. For it is in this God-given power to speak, to utter syllables and to frame them into intelligible means of communication with other people that we have one of the truly distinguishing human traits which separates us from the beasts.

In medieval Jewish philosophy, man is called *medaber,* "the one who speaks," for it is this faculty which differentiates us from the rest of the animal kingdom as well as from the world of nature.

What care should, therefore, be exercised in our manner of using words! Who does not know their fateful power.

Three times a day, at the end of each *Amidah*, we pray: "O God, keep my tongue from evil and my lips from speaking deceit." It is a prayer we all need to live by.

On Being Fully Alive

SOME YEARS AGO a religious sect adopted as its motto these words: "Millions now living will never die," whereupon one observer remarked, "Yes, but the tragedy is that millions now living are already dead but do not know it."

The rabbinic teachers may have been pointing in the same direction in their comment on the opening verse of this *Sidrah*.

Alluding to the deaths of the two sons of Aaron, Nadav and Avihu, the Sages said that they had suffered a peculiar kind of death: "Their souls were consumed; their bodies remained intact."

Had the Sages filled out the coroner's report, it might have read: "Biologically sound, spiritually dead." The ancient rabbis confirmed here a moral verdict that they rendered more explicitly in another passage: "The wicked even in life are considered dead."

Much is being written these days on the question of when death sets in. When the heart stops beating? When the brain stops functioning? But what is the status of the human being when the soul shrivels and the spirit withers?

At a time when there is growing popular interest in a belief in life after death and a widely publicized book is entitled, *Life After Life*, should we not each give more attention to the question "How about life during life?" Are we truly and fully alive, not only biologically, but spiritually, too?

Sinclair Lewis was a professed atheist. Once he engaged in a public debate in Kansas City on whether God exists. He finished his presentation with the dramatic challenge: "If there is a God, let him strike me dead now." He waited a few moments, nothing happened and he marched triumphantly off the platform.

The following morning the *Kansas City Times* printed an editorial response to Lewis. Of course, it said, God did strike Lewis dead even though he did not seem to be aware of it. His spiritual demise was reflected in his despair about the value of life, in his cynical contempt for people, in his sneering egotism and in his waning literary powers. It was another case of a human being biologically sound, spiritually dead.

A wise man once blessed his young grandson in these words: "My child, may you live all the days of your life."

To live all the days of our lives means to keep our minds alive, to be open to new ideas, to entertain challenging doubts, nurture a lively curiosity and strive constantly to keep learning.

To live all the days of our lives means to keep our hearts alive, to deepen our compassion, add to our friendships, retain a buoyant enthusiasm, grow more sensitive to the beauty of the world and to the wonder and the miracle of being part of it.

To live all the days of our lives means to keep our souls alive, to grow more responsive to the needs of others, more resistant to consuming greed, more nourishing of our craving for fellowship , more devoted to truth and integrity.

To live all the days of our lives means to keep our spirits alive, to face the future with confidence, secure in the knowledge that we can meet every challenge with fortitude, emerge with honor and be enriched by every experience.

To live all the days of our lives means to keep our faith alive, to remain rooted in a rich heritage, to be sustained by worship, and strengthened by a community from which we draw abiding kinship, and to which we lovingly bring the finest fruits of our minds and hearts.

Let us bring all our energies to bear upon the rewarding and exhilarating task of fully living all the days of our lives.

Where Is Holiness?

THE WORDS "holy" and "holiness" are dead tired from overwork in sermons and prayers but they are almost completely unemployed in our everyday speech. If these words are not part of our daily vocabulary, it is because the ideas they conjure up are remote from our thinking. Perhaps if we understood them better we would see a closer connection between these words and our lives. What does holiness mean?

First, let us say what holiness is not. It is not something available to the few, to the select, to spiritual leaders. It is accessible to all. Nor is holiness achieved by turning one's back on society and the world. It is achieved in the midst of daily living. Holiness is not something apart from life, it is a part of life.

The Jewish conception of holiness is revealed most clearly in the nineteenth chapter of Leviticus. There we read: "Speak to the whole congregation of the children of Israel and say to them: 'Ye shall be holy; for I, the Lord your God, am Holy' " (Lev. 19:2). Notice that the whole congregation, every Jew, is summoned to holiness.

The Bible then proceeds to teach us that holiness is not an abstract or mystic idea; it is meant to be a principle which regulates our daily lives. How is holiness attained? By honoring parents, observing the Sabbath, doing kindness to the needy, paying wages promptly, dealing honestly in business, refraining from talebearing, loving one's neighbor, showing cordiality to the stranger, and acting justly.

Holiness is the crucial dimension of daily living. One employer caught some of this spirit when he said to a prospective employee: "I see that you have references from three ministers. We don't work here on Sundays. Do you have a reference from someone who sees you on weekdays?"

Prof. Solomon Schechter, one of the great Jewish scholars of the twentieth century, once asked: "Where are the Jewish saints? In other communions, you have a long list of saints. Churches are named after saints. Where are the Jewish saints?"

Schechter answered his own question: "Jewish saints do not form a sect apart. You find them in the very midst of the community. They are not raised on a special pedestal, because a man who works as a doctor can be a saint, a man who works as a laborer can be a saint. It is sometimes possible even to achieve a degree of holiness in the pulpit—surprising as that may be."

It is this Jewish conception of holiness which found expression in the following passage included in a new High Holy Day Prayer Book, *Mahzor Hadash:*

> "There is holiness when we strive to be true to the best we know.
> There is holiness when we are kind to someone who cannot possibly be of service to us.
> There is holiness when we promote family harmony.
> There is holiness when we forget what divides us and remember what unites us.
> There is holiness when we are willing to be laughed at for what we believe in.
> There is holiness when we love—truly, honestly, and unselfishly.
> There is holiness when we remember the lonely and bring cheer into a dark corner.
> There is holiness when we share—our bread, our ideas, our enthusiasms.
> There is holiness when we gather to pray to Him who gave us the power to pray."

"In our time," wrote Dag Hammarskjöld, "the road to holiness necessarily passes through the world of action."

For us Jews that is where the road to holiness has always been.

Our Unique Privilege

SOME YEARS AGO I was called to officiate at the funeral service of a humble woman who had lived a hard life. She had stretched her husband's very meager earnings far enough to get her children educated. In the process she had severely denied herself, and she had even engaged in helping people poorer than herself. Death claimed a brilliant son just as he reached his prime. Somewhere, somehow she found the courage to go on.

When she died the newspaper carried only a paid notice. There was nothing "newsworthy" in her life or death. But one of the reasons why I remember her was because of this little detail in her life. During the depression she devoted much of her energies to providing coal for needy families, and when she would bring the coal to the cold home, she never delivered it through the front of the house. To avoid publicizing her act of kindness and also exposing the recipient to any possible loss of respect, she would deliver the coal through the back of the house.

Every year when the Torah reading cycle reaches this *Sidrah*, I think of that saintly Jewish mother, one of those little pegs that keeps this fragile world of ours from shattering.

The opening verse of this Torah portion declares: "And the Lord said unto Moses: 'Speak unto the priests, the sons of Aaron, and speak unto them . . .' " (Lev. 21:1).

The ancient Sages questioned the repetition of the word "speak."

The purpose of the apparent redundancy, they said, was to caution the prominent people about *how* they speak to the humble people. "We warn the 'big' people not to speak disdainfully to the 'little' people."

In my mind that mother became a symbol of the "little people" our Sages worried about. And in their concern for the "little people" the Sages were emulating the Almighty Himself of whom we say every morning in our prayers that He cares profoundly about the oppressed, the hungry, the burdened, the stranger, the orphan, the widow.

And this concern for the "little people" became one of the distinguishing hallmarks of our tradition. When Rabbi Israel Salanter became ill one *Erev Pesah*, he was unable to supervise the baking of the Matzot, and someone was therefore appointed to take his place. His replacement came to Rabbi Salanter to ask if he had any special instructions for him. "Yes," said the Rabbi, "there is one very important precaution I want to impress upon you. The woman who bakes the Matzot is a widow. Be especially careful how you talk to her."

If the whole truth be told, despite our Sages' use of the words "*gedolim*" and "*ketanim*"—"big people" and "little people"—they never really believed in such categories at all. In Judaism we are each a reflection of divinity, each a bearer of the divine image. "There is no great and no small to the soul that maketh all."

And every one of us can aspire to greatness. Greatness is measured not by fame, wealth, status, or power. Some of the most heroic people we all have known have been unsung and untrumpeted. We have known parents who have cared for a handicapped child day after day, week after week, and year after year, compensating for nature's frail endowment with massive doses of inexhaustible love.

We have known young mothers who have borne bravely the heavy burden of widowhood and managed to be both mother and father to their children.

In recent years I have witnessed in a geriatric center the unflagging uncomplaining heroism of some children who devote themselves for years to the comfort of parents who are no longer even aware of the sacrificial devotion being lavished upon them.

We have all known humble people of whom fame has never even heard who have a boundless capacity for bringing cheer into lonely lives, who are drawn by some special instinct to human need, who are always scrubbing the little corner assigned to them to make it brighter and cleaner.

A few years ago the man who served as the White House stenographer for thirty years retired. During a press interview he was asked which of the presidents for whom he had worked he would rate highest. "President Truman" was his prompt reply. "He was the only president who knew who I was and called me by my name."

That stenographer rated the "big" people by how they related to the "little" people. It's a fairly good measuring rod to determine a person's true size.

Creeds and Deeds

ONE OF THE most risky real estate deals in history is described in this week's prophetic portion. The piece of land was in Jerusalem. What made the purchase so speculative was the timing.

The year was 586 before the Common Era, and Jerusalem was under an unbreakable siege by the powerful Babylonian armies. The destruction of the city and the exile of its inhabitants were imminent. Indeed, Jeremiah himself had predicted these events and had gotten himself thrown into prison for his efforts.

At this perilous time, God advises Jeremiah to purchase a plot of land. This land was a field in the city of Anatot, and it was the property of Hanamel, the son of his father's brother. Hanamel was apparently compelled by circumstances to sell it, and according to the prevailing Biblical law, Jeremiah as a kinsman was obliged to purchase the field so that it should not pass from the family.

But the purchase of the field at this particular time would have, in addition, a crucial symbolic significance. It would dramatically give expression to the faith that after the destruction and exile which were now unavoidable, there would be return and rebirth.

But how can Jeremiah convince the people not to despair? How can they be persuaded to cling to so frail and fragile a hope? Only one way. Buy the field. Risk some silver and save a people. Jeremiah's personal faith in his people's future restoration would be of little consequence unless he acted on that faith.

A truth leaps at us from this dramatic transaction. The value of our beliefs is reflected in how we behave. Our convictions become concrete where they are converted into conduct. Our creeds become vital when they shape our deeds.

An interesting historical parallel to Jeremiah's purchase is found centuries later during Hannibal's invasion of Italy. At that critical time one Roman patriot bought at full price in public auction the ground on which Hannibal's army was encamped.

A somewhat similar gesture of faith in our own people's future came to the surface following the Six Day War in June 1967. The first major cultural event following the conclusion of the war was a concert on the recently recaptured Mount Scopus.

One of the passengers on the bus which climbed Mount Scopus gave the driver a ticket he had purchased in 1948 before Mount Scopus had been captured by the Arabs. He had held on to the ticket for nineteen years, confident that he would one day be able to use it.

So many of our beliefs lie asleep in the quiet dormitory of our minds. They never awake in action. Little wonder that they matter so little.

A national poll a while ago showed that the overwhelming majority of Americans believe in God. But when they were asked whether it made any difference in their behavior more than half said it did not.

These figures justify the complaint of Dr. Melvin E. Wheatley: "Great hosts of people worship a God of religion who is not at all the God of all life. He is a pious presence in the sacraments but an impudent intruder in the science lab. He is a point of reference for prayers, but an unemployed consultant on business contracts."

Religion, to be alive, must be acted out in the arena of life. Its concern is not only to keep the Sabbath holy, but to keep the weekdays honest.

One of our teachers at the rabbinical seminary cautioned us that the feast of the sermon is always followed by spiritual indigestion unless it is followed by religious exercise. And then he added: "Remember, one kind act will teach more love of God than a thousand sermons."

The matter was summed up best by a prophet whose literary remains are only three chapters in our Bible. But he put us in his everlasting debt in three Hebrew words which are translated: "The righteous shall live by his faith" (Hab. 2:4).

"If"

THE TORAH PORTION of this week begins with the tiny word "if," which plays such a massive role in our lives. "If" is a little hinge on which the door of destiny swings. A history professor built an impressive case in defense of the observation that if Cleopatra's nose had been one inch longer, the entire history of the world would have been different.

The very structure of the word "life" is a reminder of the vast contingencies with which it is fraught. In the middle of the word *life* there is *if*. In the middle of every life there is a big *if*.

The celebrated artist Whistler had his heart set upon a career in the army, but he flunked out of West Point because he failed in chemistry. In later life, he used to say: "If silicon had been a gas, I would have been a major general."

There is indeed a big *if* in the middle of every life. What if . . . if I had married a different woman, if I attended a different school, if I had chosen a different career . . .

Robert Frost makes this point sharply in a haunting little poem called "The Road Not Taken." Once, while walking through the forest, he came upon a fork where two paths branched out. Naturally, he could take only one of them, but in the poem he wonders what would have happened had he taken the other path. The path he did take, he concludes, "has made all the difference."

Nor is it only our own choices and our own decisions that affect our destinies. During the Nazi Holocaust, when European Jewry was being decimated, many of us asked ourselves: "What if my father had not made the boat?" Our very lives hinged upon a decision made by our fathers, who could not possibly have been aware at the time of the fateful consequences of their choice.

Despite all the uncertainties and the unpredictable contingencies of life, we have to accept it as it is and live it the best way we know. We cannot go through life second-guessing ourselves or wishing that things were other than they are.

In his autobiography, *My Young Years*, the master pianist Artur Rubinstein addressed himself directly to this matter. "Most people," he wrote, "have an unrealistic approach toward happiness because they invariably use the fatal conjunction 'if' as a condition. You hear them say: I would be happy *if* I were rich or *if* this woman loved me, or *if* I had talent, or the most popular 'if'—*if* I had good health. They often attain their goal, but then they discover new 'if's.

"As for myself, I love life for better or for worse, unconditionally."

Perhaps it was this capacity to love life "unconditionally" that enabled Rubinstein to enjoy such a long and fruitful life. But what he calls "the fatal conjunction" does have a crucial role in our lives. We may choose to love life unconditionally, but life itself is full of conditions.

We live in a world of cause and effect, where every action has a reaction. If we want certain results, we must fulfill certain conditions.

This is the central thrust of this week's *Sidrah*, which begins with "if." *If* you follow the commandments, then there will be serenity and fulfillment. ". . . and you shall lie down and none shall make you afraid." But if you reject the commandments and break the covenant, then there will be misery and suffering. ". . . and you shall flee when none pursues you."

It was this passage and several others like it in the Torah that prompted my revered teacher, Professor Mordecai Kaplan, to observe that "Judaism is neither pessimistic nor optimistic; it is *if*istic." It tells us what we can make of our lives *if* we fulfill certain conditions.

This is not a haphazard universe. It is a universe governed by law, and in the moral realm as in the physical realm, nature can be commanded only by being obeyed.

If we want a harvest, we have to plant seeds. If we want good health, we have to follow a program of diet, exercise and self-control that leads to good health. If we want friendship, we must perform acts of friendship. If we want to live serenely, we have to live morally. To be sure, there are some ifs over which we have no control, but in so many crucial areas of life, we, and we alone, do have control.

The Internal Revenue Service received an envelope containing $1,000 in cash and an unsigned note that read: "I am sending you this money because I cannot sleep. If I still cannot sleep, I will send you more."

The sender of that note reminds us of a truth we frequently suppress. Much of what we call insomnia is the work of an offended conscience getting even. The "still small voice" has a nasty way of becoming shrill and raspy just when we're trying to get some sleep.

At such times, we can appreciate one of the rewards the Torah promises us for keeping the commandments—"and you shall lie down and none shall make you afraid."

What the Torah is promising here is built into our very structure as human beings. God so fashioned us that we cannot betray our highest principles with impunity. And when we do indeed live in the way He would have us live and we know we should live, we experience the joy and inner happiness that enrich life, add zest to it and keep it sweet to our taste.

It is worth noting that the Hebrew word for life is also a four-letter word. It is *hayyim*. But unlike its English counterpart, which has *if* in the middle of it, the Hebrew word for life has two *yuds* in the middle. And two *yuds*, as we know, spell the name of God.

If we put God in the vital center of our lives, we can meet any contingency without being defeated or overwhelmed. And we can then live with the certainty that life has meaning, purpose and unlimited possibilities for fulfillment.

Finding God in the Wilderness

THE FOURTH BOOK of the Torah is called *Bemidbar,* which means "in the wilderness." The book is largely devoted to the vicissitudes our ancestors endured during those difficult years when they journeyed through the wilderness of Sinai toward the Promised Land that beckoned ahead.

Those years in the wilderness were extraordinarily hazardous. Nature and man conspired so severely against the recently liberated slaves that they often wished they were back in Egypt. There was hunger and there was thirst, there were marauding desert tribes who lived by plunder. The burning sand and sun blistered them by day, the cold desert winds froze them at night. The wilderness was most uncongenial to human habitation. It was fierce, harsh, dangerous.

And yet this book begins with the simple but startling statement: "And the Lord spoke to Moses in the wilderness of Sinai." There in that wasteland, there in the midst of the most perilous terrain and circumstances, God speaks. And not to Moses alone. Indeed, God's most dramatic self-revelation was heard by the entire people in the wilderness of Sinai. Whatever the wilderness was, it was not "God-forsaken." Even there His voice could be heard.

Is there not something profoundly instructive in this phenomenon? Does it not seem to suggest to us that even in life's most forbidding circumstances, or perhaps especially then, we can hear

God's voice and feel His presence? Human experience daily confirms this striking truth.

Harry Emerson Fosdick was one of America's greatest preachers and teachers of the reality of God. This is generally acknowledged. What is not too well known is the rocky path by which he climbed to spiritual eminence. When he was a young man he suffered a severe nervous breakdown. Looking back to that terrible time in his life he wrote in later years:

"It was the most terrifying wilderness I ever traveled through. I dreadfully wanted to commit suicide, but instead I made some of the most vital discoveries of my life. My little book, *The Meaning of Prayer*, would never have been written without that time of mourning and grief. I found God in a desert. Why is it that some of life's most revealing insights come to us not from life's loveliness, but from life's difficulties? As a small boy said, 'Why are all the vitamins in spinach and not in ice cream, where they ought to be?' I don't know. You will have to ask God that, but vitamins are in spinach and God is in every wilderness."

Yes, God is in every wilderness but not all people who are in the desert of tribulation hear Him speak. Quite often people turn against God when they are confronted by sickness, tragedy, or the loss of loved ones. Which rabbi has not heard people say: "When my mother died I stopped believing in God. She was so good, how could something so dreadful happen to her?" Who can dare to estimate how many atheists were created by the Holocaust?

And yet who will deny that there are survivors whose faith in God was either discovered or strengthened in the wilderness of anguish during the black night of incarceration? Reeve Robert Brenner in his excellent book *The Faith and Doubt of Holocaust Survivors* reports the following statement of one survivor: "When I hear of other survivors who say they became atheists because of the death of the six million, I become very excited and angry and I always let them know that it is precisely because of the six million that I became a religious Jew, keeping the commandments and developing in myself a deep faith in God. The six million sacrificed so much, their very lives. How can you betray them again after they've gone by using their death as a justification for becoming a *goy* . . . ?"

It is one of life's astonishing paradoxes that we often see more clearly when our eyes are dimmed by tears. In the arid desert soil of suffering there often grow tender shoots of compassion, sympathy and service. Sorrow has played a transforming role in the lives of countless bereaved who could say in a mood of melancholy gratefulness with Wordsworth: "A deep distress hath humanized my soul."

When we ourselves experience suffering we can become more sensitive to the suffering of others. After all, sooner or later do we not all find ourselves in life's wilderness? Does all our vaunted power, prestige and affluence immunize us against those "shafts of outrageous fortune" which are our common destiny?

The wilderness can elicit from us powers of fortitude, patience and endurance. It can strip away our pettiness, our pride, our self-centeredness. It can puncture our illusions of invulnerability and self-sufficiency. It can make us more profoundly aware than ever before how great is our dependence upon Him who, in the words of Isaiah, "gives power to the faint, and to him who has no might He increases strength."

In the wilderness of sorrow we often begin to understand what the Biblical Joseph meant when he said: "God has made me fruitful in the land of my affliction." We understand better too the more profound meaning of what the Torah tells us about Moses: "And Moses entered into the thick darkness for there was God." And we understand also why Chateubriand, the unbeliever, said after the death of his sister: "I wept and then I believed." Again and again God has been found in the desert.

In Israel we saw a rare cactus plant on which there grows an exquisitely lovely flower. That flower is called *Malkat Halailah*—Queen of the Night—because it has the strange characteristic of blooming only in the darkest part of the night. When the blackness is deepest, the *Malkat Halailah* comes bursting out. We can emulate that flower. In the dark night of suffering and sorrow we can hear God's voice calling to us to robe ourselves in our full human splendor, bedecked in all our God-given glory.

Painting Peace

~~~ ⚜ ~~~

ONE OF THE most widely known and most frequently quoted passages from the Hebrew Bible is the priestly blessing that we read in this *Sidrah:*

> "The Lord bless you and keep you,
> The Lord deal kindly and graciously with you.
> The Lord bestow His favor upon you and grant you peace."
> (Num. 6:24-26.)

The threefold blessing climaxes with "peace." The Hebrew word for peace is *Shalom.* Jews greet one another with *Shalom;* it means both hello and goodby. So precious is peace that one Talmudic Sage went so far as to declare: "The name of the Holy One, blessed be He, is 'Shalom!' "

For us who live in the post-Hiroshima period it is imperative that we rededicate ourselves to the relentless search for peace. But even as we do so, we ought to be warned that there are all kinds of phony pretenders which masquerade as peace.

It is easy enough to declare ourselves for peace, to pray for it and to extol it. It is also easy, however, to pervert the meaning of peace as many dictators have done. They act in the spirit of Joe in the anecdote. His friend asked him: "You say you are a lover of peace, Joe. Then why did you throw the brick at John?"

"Because," Joe answered, "after I threw the brick, John was at peace."

Peace may be too dearly purchased. When Neville Chamberlain returned from Munich after selling out Czechoslovakia to Hitler, he proudly announced that he had secured "peace in our time." Never was a statesman more self-deluded. The greater tragedy was that he also helped to delude the Western world and to lull it into a false and very fragile sense of security.

Peace may either be bought or it may be won. It is bought by compromise with evil. It is won by resistance to evil. Much as we love peace, we ought not to be so mushy in our thinking that peace at any price become the ultimate goal. Peace is inseparable from justice, from freedom and from human dignity.

The elusiveness of peace is perhaps most vividly revealed in this shocking statistic. In all the 5000 years of recorded history there have been only 128 years when there was no war being fought somewhere on the face of the earth.

For us this is small consolation, because never before have nations been armed with such massive destructive power.

When Winston Churchill heard the news of Hiroshima he said: "Safety will be the child of terror, and survival the twin of annihilation." Today that statement is no longer true. If anything it is misleading. Today a nuclear holocaust offers neither hope for safety nor survival.

In his widely acclaimed *The Fate of the Earth,* Jonathan Schell graphically spelled out in gruesome and chilling detail the possible consequences of a nuclear conflagration.

A single megaton bomb would devastate an area of more than 100 square miles, create winds of 400 miles an hour and launch a fireball that would consume all living things in its path. It would burn up the oxygen in the air and create toxic gases that within 24 hours would kill those who took refuge in shelters.

A single 20-megaton bomb—of which the United States and the Soviet Union each have more than 100—would have 1600 times the power of the bomb that hit Hiroshima. It would burn up and disintegrate every structure over an area of 450 square miles. Its blast would be felt over an area of 1400 square miles. Its fireball, over 4 miles in diameter, would kill everything within 20 miles and would blind everyone within hundreds of miles.

A single 10,000 megaton attack which both superpowers are now capable of launching, would be the equivalent of 800,000 Hiroshimas!

The fate of the earth itself would be doomed.

There simply could be no winners in a nuclear war.

Place alongside these gruesome facts these condemning statistics: The nations of the world spend $1.3 million on arms every minute. In that same minute, 30 children die for want of food and inexpensive vaccines. The cost of a single nuclear submarine equals the annual education budget of 23 developing countries with 160 million school children.

As we think on these things, we must renew our determination to pursue true peace with all the strength, all the imagination and all the zeal at our command.

Perhaps the time has come for our government, which has a war department, to add a peace department, a body of men and women whose sole task it would be to explore every idea, every avenue, every instrument to further peace in the world.

In our more vigorous pursuit of peace, perhaps we might find some inspiration in a poem written by thirteen-year-old Tali Sorek, from Beersheba, Israel.

> "I had a box of colors—
> Shining, bright and bold.
> I had a box of colors,
> Some warm, some very cold.
>
> I had no red for the blood of wounds.
> I had no black for the orphans' grief.
> I had no white for dead faces and hands.
> I had no yellow for burning sands.
>
> But I had orange for the joy of life,
> And I had green for buds and nests.
> I had blue for bright, clear skies.
> I had pink for dreams and rest.
>
> I sat down and painted Peace."

Bigness Versus Greatness

THE PROPHETIC READING of this week contains one verse that rabbis take special delight in using as a text for their sermons. The verse appears in the Book of Zechariah: "Not by might, nor by power, but by My Spirit, says the Lord of Hosts" (4:6).

The verse extols the supremacy of spiritual power over physical power, and thus seems to validate the strong pacifistic element in the Jewish tradition.

Significantly, this same prophetic portion is read on the Sabbath of Hanukkah where it seems to fly in the face of the central event that made Hanukkah possible. If there is any holiday on the Jewish calendar which celebrates military might, it is Hanukkah. After all, the rededication of the Temple occurred only because the Maccabees succeeded in vanquishing the Syrians on the field of battle and thereby recapturing the holy Temple that the enemy had defiled. Without military valor there would have been no miracle to celebrate and no Hanukkah.

How profoundly paradoxical then, that on the holiday which owes its very existence to might and power triumphant we should read the pacifistic put-down by the prophet: "Not by might, nor by power, but by My spirit, says the Lord of Hosts."

Nor is this verse likely to capture any popularity prizes among contemporary world leaders. At a time when billions are being spent on armaments by rich and poor nations alike, when nations buy missiles before they build schools and hospitals—at such a time the words of the prophet seem too removed from the world of reality to be taken seriously. The mood of our time was perhaps captured more precisely by Mao Tse-tung when he said: "Every communist must grasp the truth that power grows out of the barrel of a gun."

Because the words of the prophet seem so remote from our way of thinking, they merit special emphasis. Their truth, however unpopular, is worth considering.

The history of the Jewish people provides a dramatic illustration of Zechariah's teaching. The Jews have outlived great and powerful empires which once strutted noisily and arrogantly across the stage of history. Their conquering armies, their massive might did not rescue them from oblivion. The Jew witnessed their rise and their fall, their coming and their going, while he was armed only with his Torah, his traditions, his faith.

Moreover, the Jew has enriched the larger human family very disproportionately with the gifts of his spirit. David Lloyd George could therefore say with much justification, "God has chosen little nations as the vessels by which he carries his choicest wines to the lips of humanity, to rejoice their hearts, to exalt their vision, to strengthen their faith."

Having said all this by way of illustrating the truth of Zechariah's teaching we have to be frank enough to admit that it is not the whole truth. A convincing case can be made for the exorbitant cost of physical powerlessness. What an awesome price in life and treasure we Jews have paid down the centuries for our vulnerability. The Crusades, the expulsions, the inquisitions, the pogroms and ultimately the devastating Holocaust are all the result of Jewish defenselessness. We were fair game because we could be attacked with impunity by mobs, rulers and ecclesiasts.

One has only to read Bialik's outraged reaction to the Kishinev pogroms to appreciate the terrible consequences of our passivity. In his *City of Slaughter* he excoriates "the descendants of the Maccabees" who hid in cellars like cowards while their homes were plundered, their women were being violated. That poem did much to create a Jewish resistance movement which in turn fathered the Haganah and ultimately became the core of Israel's defense forces.

Abba Eban is a dove in the spectrum of Israeli politics. And yet it was he who pointed out with much reluctance that the three most important events in contemporary Jewish history were each made possible by military means. Those were the defeat of Hitler, the birth of the State of Israel, and Sadat's decision to make peace with Israel. Sadat did not come to Jerusalem because he was persuaded of the moral validity of Zionism. He would have much preferred a Middle East from which Israel had been eliminated. Sadat signed a peace treaty with Israel because his defeat in the Yom Kippur War, which he started with everything in his favor, convinced him that Israel could not be vanquished militarily. He would have to live with a State of Israel.

What then are we to do with the ringing challenge of Zechariah not to rely on might and power? If we interpret them to require that we disarm militarily, we as Jews and as Americans would be inviting destruction in a dangerous world. But his words can, however, warn us against total reliance on military prowess. Perhaps we should read his words to counsel: *"Not* by might *alone,* nor by power *alone,* but *also* by My spirit . . . "

His words can challenge us to attempt to match our physical strength with a corresponding spiritual strength. Power must be redeemed by purpose and elevated by principle.

What Adlai Stevenson said of America is intimately related to our point. "If we win men's hearts throughout the world, it will not be because we are a big country but because we are a great country. Bigness is imposing, but greatness is enduring."

The enduring power of any country resides in its belief in human dignity, its commitment to justice and dignity, its practice of freedom and equality.

It is in this way that a country and a people live "by My spirit." And it is to that spirit that Napoleon paid tribute in the latter years of his life. Though he is remembered best for his military campaigns, the words he spoke to his minister of education are an eloquent affirmation of Zechariah's teaching. "Do you know, Fontaine, what astonishes me most in this world is the inability of force to create anything. In the long run the sword is always beaten by the spirit."

On Facing Facts

THE JEWISH CAPACITY for independence of thought has become almost proverbial. It has given birth to a number of quips. One has it that the only thing two Jews can agree on is how much a third Jew should give to charity. Another piece of popular folklore is that where there are two Jews there are usually three opinions.

We therefore should hardly be surprised that there was no unanimity among the twelve spies that Moses sent to determine whether the Land of Canaan could be conquered by the Israelites.

A small minority of two—Joshua and Caleb—reported that the land could indeed be conquered. The rest said no, this is mission impossible. "The cities are impregnable; their inhabitants are giants."

Unhappily, the people were understandably impressed by the size of the majority, and consequently suffered from a failure of nerve. This generation would therefore not be the one to enter the Promised Land. A new generation would have to arise, uncrippled by defeatism, and that generation would dare to conquer.

However depressing this Biblical incident is, it has at least one redeeming feature. All twelve of the spies had the courage to face the facts. That their interpretation of the facts differed was unfortunate —and perhaps not unexpected. But face the facts they all did.

As I reread this episode in the early history of our ancestors, I recalled an incident that took place much closer to home. When the movie "Oh, God" was shown, a church in Watertown, New York, posted pickets outside the theater because, they said, it is "blasphemous, sinful, and a mockery."

Their minister was quoted in the newspaper report as objecting to the movie because it would lead to other films that depict God "as a pervert and a revolutionist."

I saw the movie "Oh, God" twice. The first time I went at the encouragement of some friends whose opinions I value. The second time I went to make careful notes on the dialogue because I had decided to discuss the film on the pulpit. In addition, I then read the book on which the movie was based.

I found "Oh, God" delightful entertainment, expounding in the main an excellent theology and a most acceptable standard of morality. My purpose now, however, is not to record my disagreement with the Watertown pickets and their minister. This is, as they say, a free country and as in the case of the twelve spies, perceptions differ.

But what shrieked at me from the newspaper story was this quote from the minister: "We have not seen the movie—we don't have to." Never saw the movie and called out the pickets! Never saw the movie and is predicting all kinds of terrible consequences.

Here's a man whose mind is made up and he doesn't want to be confused by the facts. He justifies the definition someone once gave of prejudice—"a labor-saving device." It enables one to form opinions without bothering to dig up the facts.

Perhaps as a Jew I am especially sensitive to the dangers inherent in this kind of opinion forming without reference to reality. As history's most persistent victim of every variety of vicious slander, the Jew knows only too well how many rivers of blood have flowed because cruel myths were accepted and basic facts were disregarded. People who believed absurdities committed atrocities.

The world becomes a very treacherous place when we condemn movies we haven't seen or people we haven't met.

I frequently think with gratitude of another minister who was a classmate in the Army Chaplain's School during World War II. One morning as several Jewish chaplains were emerging from services, he approached us and said somewhat apologetically: "I hope you fellows won't mind taking off your hats and posing for a picture. I'd like to send it home to my parishioners to prove to them that Jews don't have horns." We posed for the picture. Call off the pickets.

Contempt for facts has also been one of the most formidable obstacles to progress. When Galileo discovered the satellites of Jupiter, a self-styled astronomer named Sizzi refuted Galileo's claim in a manner worthy of our Watertown pickets. He argued that because there were seven openings in the human head—two ears, two nostrils, two eyes and a mouth—and seven days of the week, and seven metals, then there must be only seven planets. Otherwise, he claimed, "the whole beautiful system falls to the ground." Instead of playing a game of numbers, all he had to do was look up at the evidence, but his mind was like concrete—all mixed up and permanently set. Call out the pickets.

Before Chaim Weizmann became the first president of the State of Israel, he was once at a party conversing with the wife of a diplomat when the lady suddenly said: "Dr. Weizmann, I must apologize to you." "Apologize for what?" Weizmann asked in surprise. "Why, we have just met." "That's just it," she answered. "I want to apologize for what I thought of you before I met you."

You shall know the facts and the facts shall make you free from prejudice.

The Gifts We Withhold

UNDER THE INFLUENCE of the TV presentation of "Roots" one young man developed a burning desire to learn his own geneology. However he lacked the necessary funds to engage someone to perform this service for him. Whereupon he consulted a wise friend and asked him if he knew a way that he could have his family background traced without money. "That's easy," his friend assured him, "all you have to do is run for public office."

Those who aspire to leadership must be prepared to have their past meticulously scrutinized under a probing microscope. And that is not all. As we read in the case of Moses in this *Sidrah*, leaders must also be prepared to have their motives impugned, their integrity questioned and even their right to lead radically challenged.

Such a challenge to Moses' leadership was led by Korah. Some of the charges he leveled against Moses are cited in the Torah itself. Our Sages elaborated further on the confrontation. They pictured Korah as trying to discredit Moses by mocking his teachings.

Here is one dialogue: "You Moses have taught us 'Do not rob the poor for he is poor.' That's ridiculous! How can one possibly rob from the poor? Since he is poor there is nothing to rob from him!"

To this taunt Moses replied: "Yes, it is possible to rob the poor. The charity we are obliged to give to the poor man is rightfully his. When we fail to give it to him we are indeed robbing him."

A profoundly sensitive truth is contained in the answer of Moses.

Robbing does not necessarily involve taking from another what already belongs to that person; sometimes we rob by failing to give that person what he needs. We impoverish others by the gifts we withhold from them, by the support we fail to extend. We can rob without taking. We can rob by not giving.

This kind of robbery never shows up in the crime statistics and is punishable by no court of justice. But upon reflection we realize that it is far more prevalent than we suspect. And not only where material things are concerned.

Consider, for example, how often we withhold a word of appreciation and encouragement to those who desperately need to be praised and given a lift. How quick we are to criticize, but slow to compliment. One little boy on his first day in nursery school was asked by the teacher what his name was. He replied: "Billy don't."

Thomas Carlyle's wife was a highly gifted person, one of the most clever women in England in her time. She loved her husband dearly, and to the extent that he was capable of loving any woman other than his mother, he loved her too. After her death, he read this entry in her diary: "Carlyle never praises me. If he says nothing I have to be content that things are all right."

He had been living for decades with a woman whose heart hungered and ached for a word of appreciation—a word which this prolific writer of words had never been kind enough to utter. Did he not rob her by failing to give her what she so much needed to have?

There is also a specifically Jewish dimension to this form of robbery. Consider, for example, Jewish parents who deny their children what rightfully belongs to them—their Jewish heritage.

Some time ago Paul Cowan, author of the book *An Orphan In History*, addressed our congregation. During the course of his remarks he spoke of the de-Judaized atmosphere in which he grew up.

His father had changed his name from Cohen to Cowan. In his parents' home they had an elaborate Christmas celebration, not a word or gesture about Hanukkah. At Easter the family gathered for a dinner of ham and sweet potatoes. Paul and his brother attended Choate, an Episcopalian prep school, where he learned stately Christian hymns and litanies by heart. Paul had no Bar Mitzvah, never entered a synagogue, and while he was growing up he doesn't remember knowing anyone who kept Kosher or observed Shabbat.

By a fortuitous combination of circumstances Paul found his own way to the heritage that had been kept from him. His book is subtitled: "Retrieving A Jewish Legacy." Though both his parents were killed in a tragic fire, he is an "orphan" no longer. Paul and his wife Rachel who converted to Judaism are active, practicing Jews.

Thus Paul writes: "There's no question that my deepening awareness of being Jewish has given me a more secure sense of my own identity. It has eased my loneliness in America by teaching me that I do have a home in a tradition I love."

As we read Paul's moving story we rejoice over his rewarding discovery of his Jewish identity and heritage. But how many Paul Cowans have not been so fortunate? How many did not retrieve their Jewish legacy? How many were robbed of their spiritual inheritance and remain Orphans in History?

Being a Jewish parent is an awesome responsibility for we are each a link between the hundred Jewish generations that have preceded us and whatever Jewish generations will follow us. Those who have gone before us have accumulated a precious legacy for us to enjoy, to enlarge and to transmit. Ours is the privilege to keep faith with the past, to give meaning to our present, to insure our future.

To fulfill these tasks we must make certain that our children receive what belongs to them—a rich, vibrant and meaningful Jewish heritage. They must never feel like "orphans." They are related to some of the tallest giants of the spirit who ever walked this earth.

Using the Past Wisely

NOSTALGIA, IT HAS been said, is when we find the present tense and the past perfect. Current difficulties cast a retroactive glow of happiness on the past, and conceal its pains and its problems. Distance in time as in space lends enchantment.

This Torah portion describes two severe attacks of nostalgia—two of many of our ancestors suffered in the wilderness. When they ran short of water or became fed up with a steady diet of manna they looked back to the "good old days" before Moses led them into this predicament.

"Why did you make us leave Egypt to die in the wilderness? There is no bread and no water, and we have come to loathe this miserable food." "We remember the fish we used to eat in Egypt free, the cucumbers and the melons and the leeks and the onions and the garlic. But now our soul is dried up; we have nothing except this manna to look to."

Oh the glory that was Egypt! The grandeur we left behind!

Conveniently edited out of their rosy memories was the degradation of slavery, the brutality of arbitrary whippings, the bricks without straw, the groans of broken bodies, the decree consigning every male Hebrew infant to death at birth. "Boy, did we have fish and cucumbers and garlic in Egypt!" Forgotten of course was the fact that these foods were flavored with bitter tears and eaten with the bread of affliction.

The tendency to romanticize the past and to denigrate the present did not begin with our ancestors in the wilderness. The oldest piece of writing in existence is a cuneiform script on a piece of papyrus some 6000 years old. It contains this complaint: "Alas, times are not what they used to be. Everyone wants to write a book and children are no longer obedient to their parents."

And when do you think the following commentary on the younger generation was written? "Our youth now love luxury, they have bad manners, contempt for authority; they show disrespect for elders, and they love to chatter instead of exercise. Children are now tyrants, not the servants of their household. They no longer rise when elders enter the room. They contradict their parents, chatter before company, gobble up their food and tyrannize their teachers."

No, this is not the report of a principal to the school board on the behavior of high school students in the inner city; it is a lament of Socrates written some 2400 years ago!

In the "good old days" they also longed for the good old days. Perhaps the best thing we can say about the good old days is that they cannot come back. If we doubt it, let's try to read this page tonight by an oil lamp.

After a lifetime of studying America's past, Otto Bettmann's verdict in 1974 was a book called *The Good Old Days—They Were Terrible*.

And let's not forget that one day the very days which now fill us with so much discontent and grumbling will one day be considered "the good old days."

Despite the nostalgia that filled our ancestors in the wilderness the whole thrust of Judaism is to look forward not backward. Our messiah has not yet come. Moses is told by the Almighty to command the complaining Israelites in the wilderness: "Sanctify yourselves for tomorrow!" The road to fulfillment leads not to yesterday but to tomorrow.

Having said all this we ought to hasten to add that if we should not deify the past neither should we denigrate it. Unless we know where we come from we do not know who we are and where we should be facing. A generation without Jewish memories is a generation without Jewish hopes. To be sure we cannot and should not live in the past; but the past can and should live in us.

In his poignant autobiography *Growing Up*, Russell Baker talks about the thoughts that came to him as a result of his visits with his bedridden mother who is in her 80's. "These hopeless end-of-the-line visits with my mother made me wish I had not thrown off my own past so carelessly. We all come from the past, and children ought to know what it was that went into their making, to know that life is a braided cord of humanity stretching up from time long gone, and that it cannot be defined by a single journey from diaper to shroud."

A moving illustration of this truth was contained in a lengthy article in the *Wall Street Journal* on the incredible scope of Jewish fundraising in America. Imbedded in the story was the account of a Jew from Washington who recently became active in Jewish affairs. During his first trip to Israel he visited Yad Vashem, the magnificent and moving Holocaust memorial in Jerusalem. "There," we are told, he "noticed a small wooden *menorah* that had been made by a doomed inmate. Since that trip, lighting the Sabbath candles has become a Friday night ritual" in his home.

This is the way to use our past to enrich our present and to guarantee our future.

Uncritical Lovers—
Unloving Critics

THE BIBLICAL character Balaam is better remembered for his talking donkey than for any of the words he himself uttered. But we may be surprised to learn that some of the most extravagant and beautiful tributes to the Israelites in our entire Bible were spoken by Balaam.

Balaam, we will recall, was believed to possess a special power. As Balak, the king of Moab, said to him: "I know that whomever you bless is blessed and whomever you curse is cursed." And since Balak dreaded the alleged military might of the approaching Israelites, he engaged Balaam to put the curse on them. Much to Balak's dismay, however, he who came to curse remained to bless.

His praise borders on the rhapsodic. "None has beheld iniquity in Jacob, neither has one seen perverseness in Israel; the Lord his God is with him . . ." And in a burst of admiration which has become the first words we utter when we enter the synagogue, Balaam exclaims: "How beautiful are your tents, O Jacob, your dwellings, O Israel!"

Now the strange thing about Balaam is the fate he suffered at the hands of the Jewish authorities in post-Biblical times. He is called *Bilam ha-rasha*, "Balaam the wicked." Why such a harsh verdict? Is this the way to treat a friend?

A *Hasidic Rebbe* gave a suggestive explanation for the unfavorable light in which the tradition regarded Balaam. His intention was not to help the Israelites but to hurt them. By lauding them so profusely he wanted to persuade them that they had already attained perfection and therefore did not need to strive to improve themselves.

Had they taken him seriously and accepted his inflated estimate of themselves they would have deteriorated and disappeared as did the other peoples the Bible mentions.

What saved the Israelites from such a fate were the stern rebukes and the strong criticisms of the prophets of Israel. Because the prophets loved their people, they sought to spur them on to ever greater achievement and they therefore never grew weary of castigating them for their moral failures and shortcomings.

The *Rebbe's* insight was echoed by Winston Churchill who once wrote in another context: "Censure is often useful, praise often deceitful."

But how many of us are philosophical enough to accept censure and criticism? The Book of Proverbs assures us: "Rebuke a wise man and he will bless you"; but how many of us bless our critics? Criticism is a blow to our ego, an assault upon our self-image. Words of criticism hurt; often they hurt longer than a physical blow. How true the Yiddish adage: "A slap passes, a word remains." We can even understand the outraged complaint of Chicago's former mayor, Richard Daley: "The press has vilified me, they have crucified me; yes, they have even criticized me!"

Hard as it is to accept criticism, it is so necessary and so beneficial. Taken seriously it can prove a great stimulus to growth. A genuine friend is not one who rehearses all our virtues. We already know them quite well, thank you. A good true friend is one who cares enough about us to call attention in a gentle way to our faults. That's a friendship worth cultivating.

What is true of us as individuals is also true of a country. A reliable measure of our loyalty is our willingness to criticize the land we love. We thrill to the patriotic fervor of Capt. Stephen Decatur who exclaimed: "My country, may she always be in the right, but my country, right or wrong!" However, we suspect that a more helpful patriotism was voiced by the American statesman Carl Schurz: "My country, may she always be in the right. If right, to be kept right, if wrong to be set right."

America, John Gardener once observed, is caught in a crossfire between its uncritical lovers and its unloving critics. The same might be said of Israel. There are those who love Israel so totally and so fervently that in their eyes Israel can do no wrong. And there are those who oppose Israel so completely that in their eyes Israel can do no right.

We heard a great deal from these unloving critics during the Lebanese incursion. So intemperate was their attack, so violent their language, so distorted their perspective, that Norman Podhoretz could amply document a charge of anti-Semitism against them.

What America needs, what Israel needs, what each of us needs, are neither uncritical lovers nor unloving critics. The uncritical lovers overlook faults. The unloving critics are blind to virtues. Truly needed are loving critics. Because they criticize out of love they bring growth and blessing. They also prove themselves worthy descendants of the prophets in whose footsteps they follow.

The Man Who Never Died

IN OUR TRADITION there is only one person who was spared the universal fate of death. That person was the Prophet Elijah who, according to the Biblical account, ascended to heaven alive in a chariot of fire. That Elijah should have been the only person so uniquely favored constitutes a supreme irony, because at one point in his tumultuous life he wanted so desperately to die.

The prophetic portion we read in our synagogues this Shabbat describes the crisis of despair and hopelessness in Elijah's life.

Elijah had run away from the wrath of the idolatrous Queen Jezebel who had vowed to kill him. On Mount Carmel, Elijah had succeeded in bringing the people back to a thunderous affirmation of faith in the One God. But his triumph was to be very brief. Jezebel was determined to take revenge on Elijah.

Now we find Elijah a fugitive in the wilderness of Beer-Sheba convinced of the failure of his mission and tasting the bitter dregs of disappointment. He has fought the Lord's battles to no avail. "I have been very jealous for the Lord, God of hosts; for the children of Israel have forsaken Your covenant, thrown down Your altars and slain Your prophets with the sword. And I, I alone am left; and they seek to take away my life."

Elijah hiding in the cave is in a black mood. He feels defeated, abandoned and cornered. We can almost sympathize with his soul-wrenching plea: "It is enough, O Lord, now take away my life."

Elijah has had it. Life has crushed him. He can't go on. Now God, just one last favor please. "Take away my life."

Yes, this is the same Elijah who, the Bible tells us, was never to die. He who at one crushing juncture had begged for death, came back from the abyss of despair to live a life which was never to taste death at all.

It seems to me that there is a powerful message here to all of us when we find ourselves overwhelmed by sorrow, heartbreak or disappointment. When we are tempted to utter the ultimate heresy: "I can't go on!" Elijah's life responds: "O yes, you can!" When we pray out of the depths: "Take away my life," Elijah's triumph over surrender commands us: "Take your life and use it!"

Thoughts of Elijah surfaced a few years ago when there appeared a newspaper account of an unsigned letter of appreciation received by a gentleman in Herkimer, New York. The sender was a woman whom he had met briefly nine years earlier on an eastbound train from California. He was returning from the Pacific theatre where he had flown 60 missions in his B-25. She had just received a war department telegram informing her that her husband had been killed in action.

When they met in the vestibule of the railroad car he did not even remotely suspect that he had interrupted her attempt to commit suicide by jumping off the speeding train. Her letter made all that quite plain now.

"February 1, 1945, that night I was on the train speeding on a journey that seemed endless. You were on the train, too, speeding to the wife you hadn't seen since the war began. I doubt if you remember me now. The girl in the black dress, sad and lonely, sitting across the aisle.

"If you hadn't come into the vestibule when you did, I'd have opened the door and jumped out. Did I thank you for that and for all the kind things you did for me?

"Two years later I married again. I have a fine husband, two wonderful children and a lovely home. To think that I am so happy now and owe it all to a stranger on the train who helped me through my darkest hours . . .

"Thanks for saving my life. I'm truly grateful."

The letter was signed only, "Sincerely."

Our anonymous widow was on the verge of a desperate irrevocable act because her world had been shattered and she had seen no possibility of ever finding happiness or even meaning in life. But after the grim, dark hours had passed, the dawn of revived hope broke, and with it came the courage to hold on and tough it out until she would find new opportunities for creative living.

Such is the reward of those who do not surrender, who hold on tenaciously, and respond heroically to the challenging Biblical summons: "And you shall choose life."

It's wondrously instructive to notice that in Hebrew the word *shahor* means "black." With the slightest change of vowels, those same Hebrew letters spell *shahar*, which means "dawn." When we are engulfed by the black night of despair it is worth remembering that if we do not give up, if we cling to the precious thread of life, the blackness will be conquered by the dawn when the sun will be aflame in the east, bright with all sorts of unsuspected possibilities.

Majoring in the Minors

MARK TWAIN once said: "Man is the only animal who's got the true religion—several of them." If the casualness and frequency with which we do things "religiously" is any indication, then Mark Twain's ironic comment contains as much truth as humor. There are, indeed, a host of activities in which we engage religiously.

We play tennis every Monday—religiously.

We play bridge every Tuesday—religiously.

We go to the theater every Wednesday—religiously.

We go to the beauty parlor every Friday—religiously.

Now, I am not objecting to any of these activities. (Unconfirmed rumors allege that I have even participated in some of them myself.) I am not even objecting to the use of the word "religiously" to convey the idea of unfailing regularity. But so often the word is used by people who perform a host of secular activities "religiously," while they fulfill their religious obligations spasmodically or not at all.

They are capable of ultimate devotion to marginal concerns but only marginal devotion to ultimate concerns. In the curriculum of their lives, the electives have become required courses. The required courses have become electives.

What one father said of his teenage daughter fits many of us uncomfortably well: "She's a good student," said the father, "but she is constantly majoring in the minors." Majoring in the minors—that's what makes so much of our living trivial and inconsequential.

If it is any solace to us we should note that we are not the first generation to get our priorities mixed up. In the Torah reading of this *Sidrah* we have a distressing reminder that our Biblical ancestors were also subject to a confusion of values.

We read that the tribes of Gad and Reuben wanted to settle on the east side of the Jordan. Moses did not object to their request but he did ask them first to join their brothers in the war for the land west of the Jordan. Thus he challenges them: "Shall your brothers go to war while you sit here?"

The tribes of Gad and Reuben are impressed by Moses' argument and they do indeed agree to join their brothers in battle. But first "we will build sheepfolds for our cattle and cities for our children."

The Rabbis in the Midrash elaborating on this conversation tell us that Moses rebuked the two tribes for putting first things second and second things first. Their primary concern was with their sheep, and their children came later. "This is no way to behave," Moses declared. "First build cities for your children and then worry about your sheep." Families first; possessions later.

We who live in far more sophisticated times might find it instructive to pause to take inventory among our own priorities and values.

Which activities do we consider a "must"? Do they include spending time with our mates and children, building a Jewish home, visiting parents, attending services, reading a Jewish book, participating in a program of Jewish study, rendering service to the community, performing acts of lovingkindness, giving *tzedakah*? Or are those the things we will do "when I have time," "when I am not so tired," "after the children grow up," "after I retire"?

We have come a long way since the days of Moses. En route we have accumulated a host of scientific discoveries, technological advances, modern gadgets. A thousand servants do our bidding at the press of a button. But with all our progress we have found little happiness, and true contentment too frequently eludes us.

We have many anxieties but few anchors, much outward security but little inward serenity, enlarged means but shrunken purposes, stronger houses but weaker homes. We travel faster but too often without a sense of direction. As someone complained: "We travel at twice the speed of sound but at half the speed of sense."

Perhaps the time has come for us to reexamine our priorities. Perhaps the time has come to live our religion—religiously.

Prisoners of Hope

OUR BIBLE has been called the world's most anti-Semitic book. This verdict is somewhat exaggerated but it does contain a disquieting amount of truth. If you want to find an exhaustive catalogue of our ancestors' sins you will find it in the pages of the Book we revere most.

A chilling illustration is the *Haftarah* of this *Sidrah*. The prophetic portion is largely from the second chapter of the Book of Jeremiah. Jeremiah is unsparing in his condemnation of the whole people. He accuses them all of ingratitude, faithlessness, wickedness, idolatry.

"As the thief is ashamed when he is found, so is the house of Israel ashamed; they, their kings, their princes, their priests and their prophets" (Jer. 2:26).

But the significant thing about this *Haftarah* is that it doesn't end on a note of rebuke. To verses from chapter two, which constitutes the bulk of the *Haftarah*, are added a single verse from chapter three and two verses from chapter four. These appended verses strike an entirely different note. They speak of Israel's return to God and the ensuing spiritual regeneration which will provide a blessing to all of humanity.

Here, as in so many places in our tradition, the message concludes not with gloom nor despair but with hope. Challenge the people, criticize them, condemn them, but don't rob them of their hope. For without hope nothing is possible; with hope nothing is impossible.

Where there is hope there is life. We must resist with all our might the counsels of cynicism and discouragement which could rob us of our most cherished hopes.

When we surrender our hopes, we surrender the possiblities of improving life, changing circumstances, or planning ahead constructively and creatively. Life itself becomes an intolerable burden if there are no wings of hope to sustain it. "Hell," wrote A. J. Cronin, "is the place where one has ceased to hope."

Picture the world community without hope. If we accept wars as inevitable, hatreds between nations built into the very fabric of human society, oppression and aggression a basic and ineradicable part of our jungle inheritance; if we consider the prophet's vision of a world community rooted in justice, living by righteousness and blessed with peace—if all that is simply the delusion of a starry-eyed idealist without any possibility of being translated into reality, then we should abandon all efforts on behalf of world peace as we exclaim: "Stop the world we want to get off!"

When Shimon Peres was Israel's minister of defense, he spoke publicly about the problems of achieving a lasting peace in the turbulent Middle East. He recalled the woman who said of her husband: "He used to be an incurable optimist—but recently he's been cured." Peres added: "Israel has not been cured and remains optimistic."

Picture the Jewish community without hope. If we accepted the verdict emanating from some quarters that there is no future for Judaism in America, that it will undergo a slow and inevitable dissolution, that Jewish ignorance, assimilation and intermarriage will continue to grow until they prove fatal—if we accept this melancholy prognosis as the last word, then all our synagogues, schools, seminars, Jewish libraries, museums, colleges, publishing houses, books, magazines, newspapers, summer camps, our Jewish homes and our vast network of Jewish charitable and cultural institutions, all these are empty monuments of futility, and the better part of wisdom would be to give up, to throw in the *tallit*, to announce to the world that the 3500-year-old drama has come to an end.

We achieve as we believe.

Picture us human beings without hope. Life without hope is hopeless. If we could not hope for a second chance when life inflicts a severe defeat on us, if we could not hope for strength when we have been betrayed, if we could not hope for healing when we have been bruised, if we could not hope for recovery when we have been bereaved, if we could not hope for eternity when the winter of our lives drives home the inescapable fact of our mortality—if in all these trials hope did not sustain us, then the burden of life would become insufferable.

To be Jews is to be what Yehudah Halevi once called us, "prisoners of hope." This is one prison from which we do not wish to be liberated. We are a people whose anthem is *Hatikvah* which means "the hope."

And because we are "prisoners of hope" we do believe in the possibility of a world community living in peace and brotherhood; we do believe in an American Jewish community distinguished by a knowledge of its heritage, loyalty to its traditions and committed to its ideals. And because we are "prisoners of hope" we permit neither failure, nor perplexity, nor sorrow, nor death to defeat us.

"Hope," it has been said, "is the promissory note of life on which the principal never matures but which pays compound interest to those who render their best services each day."

According to an old parable, on one summer night two frogs fell into a bucket of milk. The first frog, realizing the hopelessness of his situation, promptly gave up and drowned. The second frog began thrashing about furiously with all his might. The following morning the farmer was surprised to find his bucket of milk turned to butter and there was a frog sitting on the top of it.

Let us cling stubbornly to our hopes. They keep us alive.

Where Are You?

ON THE SHABBAT before Tishah be-Av the word *"Eychah,"* which means "how," haunts us like a mournful refrain of despair.

We find it first in the Torah portion itself when Moses cries out in an uncharacteristic mood of helplessness: *"How* can I bear alone the trouble of you, and the burden, and the bickering!" (Deut. 1:12).

The heavy responsibilities of leadership seem to have pushed Moses to the outer limits of his endurance. He seems to be on the brink of collapse.

"Eychah" occurs a second time in the prophetic portion of this Shabbat. Isaiah is denouncing his people's sins with all the outraged passion at his command. In the midst of his fiery denunciation he exclaims: *"How* is the faithful city become a harlot! She that was full of justice, righteousness lodged in her, but now murderers" (Is. 1:21). Here it is the moral depravity of his people that has triggered the cry of despair.

And *"Eychah"* is heard a third time in the dirge of Jeremiah who is said to have written the Book of Lamentations upon beholding the destruction of the Temple. This book which is read publicly on Tishah be-Av opens with the word *"Eychah." "How* has she become as a widow, she that was great among the nations..." (Lam. 1:1). Here it is the physical destruction of Jerusalem and the Jewish people that elicits from the prophet a maddening cry of inconsolable anguish.

What is the answer to all these "hows"? How do we confront personal exhaustion, moral decay and physical devastation?

Perhaps the answer is suggested in the very word "*Eychah*." The same Hebrew letters which spell that word can be revocalized to read "*Ayekah*" which means "Where are you?"

So in the first instance the challenge is hurled back at Moses himself.

Yes, you Moses who think you have come to the end of your rope, you who have begun to doubt your own ability to carry on, where are you?

It is very tempting to throw up your hands, to be overcome by a sense of futility. Your people have indeed exasperated you, frustrated you, and drained you. Worse! They have brought you to the treacherous point of self-doubt. And all you have labored to accomplish seems doomed to failure. You are overwhelmed by circumstances which seem too massive to control. But "*Ayekah*," where are you?

Where is the Moses, the intrepid leader of four stormy decades, who confronted the might of a Pharaoh, the rebelliousness of your people, the repeated challenges to your leadership, where is that Moses? Is this the same Moses who is now whimpering: "How can I bear alone the trouble of you, and the burden, and the bickering"? Moses, the genuine Moses, where are you?

To Isaiah's denunciation of his people's moral decadence the answer is once again "*Ayekah*," where are you Isaiah? You whose lips were purified in a heavenly vision by a fiery angel, you have heard the voice of the Lord saying, "Whom shall I send and who will go for us?" and you answered: "Here am I, send me" (Is. 7:8)— where are you now Isaiah? It is precisely for this heavy purpose that you volunteered, to risk the disfavor of your own people by crying out against their sins in the sustaining hope they might mend their ways and return to God.

And to each individual who lives at a time of social and moral depravity the probing question is addressed "Where are you?" How are things in that part of the community that you inhabit? Are you part of the solution or part of the problem? What are you contributing to the moral climate? Remember, the community is only the individual "writ large," the sum total of all the people who inhabit it. If everybody in the community behaved just like you, would it be a better or worse place to live in? Where are you?

And to the despair aroused by the devastation that Jeremiah lamented, the answer to each individual once again is: Where are you? Is wringing your hands all that you can do? Is there no response other than tears? To be sure the scene of a city and a people ravaged is cause enough to make grown men cry, but after the tears have been shed, and the heaven piercing laments have been wailed, is there nothing further that can be done? Where are you? Roll up your sleeves! There's massive rebuilding to do, there are gaping wounds to bind up, there are new hopes to nurture, new dreams to salvage out of the ashes. Where, indeed, are you?

An ancient Jewish teaching consoles us with the startling announcement that on the day the Temple was destroyed the Messiah was born. Amidst the smoking ruins our ancestors felt not the paralyzing chill of death but the invigorating breath of birth. The Messiah was born out of the ashes to lead his people forward with the stubborn hope that the dark night of despair would give way before a bright dawn of hope.

Disturbing the Comfortable

THE FIRST SHABBAT after Tishah be-Av has a special name: *Shabbat Nahamu*, The Sabbath of Comfort. It is so designated because the prophetic portion that is read in the synagogue this Shabbat begins with the words: "Comfort my people, comfort them, says your God" (Is.40:1).

One of the primary functions which Judaism performs for us is to provide comfort in sorrow and solace in times which try our souls.

Heinrich Heine alluded to this truth when he called our Bible "the medicine chest of humanity." When we are bruised and burdened, when we suffer disillusionment and despair, when we grow "tired of living and feared of dying," we can find restoring balm in the Biblical assurance that "God is near to all who call upon Him, to all who call upon Him in truth."

Any student of Jewish history knows that it was the life-giving reservoirs of strength and hope that our people found in our heritage that enabled us to survive the repeated efforts to destroy us.

In a tremendously moving essay in *Midstream* magazine (April 1983) Lisa S. Kovitch provides graphic illustrations of the sustaining power so many Jews found in their faith during the cruelest of all epochs in our history: Thus she writes:

"Though the Nazi savagery and ruthlessness in carrying out the extermination of the Jewish people in Europe could have robbed anyone of his faith in God, the evidence points overwhelmingly to the conclusion that Jews did not lose faith; belief in God and in His commandments often sustained Jews throughout the Holocaust period. And when they could no longer avoid death, their faith also enabled them to march to their deaths with a dignity that mocked everything the Nazis tried to accomplish."

But even after we have said this we have not exhausted the role which our religion should play in our lives. It should not only comfort us when we are disturbed; it should also disturb us when we are comfortable.

The prophets who could soothe with motherly compassion when their people were heartsick, could also scold with bitter condemnation when their people appeared heartless. Isaiah who called out: "Comfort my people, comfort them," was the same prophet who cried out: "Woe unto the rebellious children" (30:1).

Of course, it makes better advertising copy to promote Judaism as a comforter rather than as a disturber. Heaven knows that in these difficult days the need for comfort and solace runs deep. And there are enough things in our personal lives to disturb us without turning to our religion for additional irritants.

And yet we cannot escape the truth that when Judaism offers only serenity and contentment, when it focuses all of our attention upon our personal needs and turns its back on the rest of the world, at that point Judaism betrays its own character.

"The enemy," wrote Norman Cousins, "is any man in the pulpit . . . who is a dispenser of balm rather than an awakener of conscience. He is preoccupied with the need to provide personal peace of mind rather than to create a blazing sense of restlessness to set things right."

It is worth noting that when Jews gather in our synagogues on the holy day of Rosh Hashanah the central ritual is the sounding of the Shofar. The Shofar, as Maimonides explained it, cries out to us: "Awake from your sleep, shake off your lethargy." The Shofar is not a lullaby but an alarm clock. It does not encourage complacency; it shatters it.

These are surely days when religion should be a disturber of the peace, a goad to conscience and "a blazing sense of restlessness" to address the world's wrongs.

In a world where so many worry about overeating while two-thirds of its inhabitants worry about eating at all;

where if we were to observe a minute of silence for every man, woman and child who died of hunger-related causes in any given year, we would be standing in silence throughout the rest of this century and beyond;

where the two superpowers *each* has the equivalent of 30,000 pounds of TNT for every man, woman and child on the face of this earth;

where our rivers are being poisoned and our air polluted;

where terrorists are acclaimed as "freedom fighters";

where powerful countries publish and distribute hate literature;

where Jews languish in Russian prisons for the crime of wishing to emigrate;

where nations buy missiles and tanks before they build hospitals and schools;

where four out of every five people live under a dictatorship— in such a world our religion should be a disturber of the peace.

What is needed today is not the reassurance that "God's in His heaven and all's right with the world." Rather we need to be reminded that there's so much wrong with the world that we must try to right.

"Noble discontent," it has been said, "is the path to heaven." It is also a good way to walk the earth.

Saying Grace in a Hungry World

Dear Rabbi:

The kids in our bunk were having a discussion last night whether or not we should say *Birkat Ha-mazon* (the blessing for food), the whole camp chants after every meal at Camp Ramah. Earlier in the day, we had a discussion about the millions of people who are suffering from starvation throughout the world. Thousands die from hunger daily. We, therefore, wonder whether we should thank God, who in the words of the *Birkat Ha-mazon*, "feeds the whole world with His goodness, with lovingkindness and tender mercy . . . He provides for all His creatures whom He has created." Can we say these words without feeling hypocritical?

Love, Esther

Esther Dear,

I am answering your sensitive question on the day before we will read from the Torah the verse from which we derive the obligation to thank God for the food we eat. "When you have eaten and are satisfied, you shall thank the Lord your God . . ." (Deut. 8:10).

Our ancient Sages attributed a great deal of significance to this elementary act of gratitude expressed in the blessing for the food we eat. Indeed, in our tradition, there is a blessing to be recited for everything we enjoy in life. There is a blessing for getting up in the morning, for having clothes to wear, for being able to perform our bodily functions, for enjoying freedom. We are obligated to recite daily no fewer than 100 blessings for the many gifts a gracious God showers upon us.

In the Jewish way of looking at the world, "the earth is the Lord's and all that it contains." Therefore, one of the Rabbis in the Talmud declared, "whoever enjoys any worldly pleasure without blessing God commits a theft against Him."

All right, you say, that is what the tradition requires. But, how can we recite words which fly in the face of reality?

You are right, dear. The terrible reality is that there is a frightening amount of hunger in the world. There are more hungry people in the world today than there were people in the world 100 years ago. Up to a third of the world's children die from malnutrition and related diseases before the age of 5.

In the three minutes it will take you to read this letter, three people will die because of malnutrition. If we were to observe a minute of silence for every person who died last year of hunger-related causes we would be silent throughout this century and beyond.

In a country where overeating is a serious threat to our nation's health, and one out every four Americans is overweight, we cannot easily imagine what it means to be hungry all the time—to have hunger gnaw away at mind and body slowly and relentlessly until death is welcomed as a blessed relief.

Every hungry person rebukes us. Every emaciated child chastises us. Every life cut short by hunger accuses us.

The Hebrew word for charity is "*tzedakah*." The real meaning of that word is "justice" or "righteousness." To give bread to the hungry is not an act of generosity. It is the just and right thing to do. To withhold bread from the starving is an act of injustice and unrighteousness.

Getting back to your letter, I would urge you and your bunk-mates to continue to say the words you question.

When we thank God who provides food for the entire world in His goodness, what we are saying is that God has created enough food for all His creatures. He has made the world habitable for us.

It is we who divert our resources from life-giving to life-destroying purposes. It is we who pay our farmers for not producing wheat and fruit. By affirming God's goodness in providing food for all, we rededicate ourselves to making that fact a reality.

It would seem to me that instead of abandoning this prayer, it ought to be said even louder and louder until that blessed day comes when everybody will be able to say the *Birkat Ha-mazon* in a world where none will go hungry and God's bounty will be used as He intended it. Let's all work to bring that day soon.

Thank you so much for writing.

Love, Rabbi

To Choose One's Own Way

ONE OF THE most harrowing moments in contemporary literature is the one which gives William Styron's novel its title. It is the moment describing Sophie's choice, the most horrible choice a mother could be asked to make—which of her two children to turn over to Nazi destruction and which to keep alive.

"I can't choose! I can't choose!" she screams again and again in a voice louder than "hell's pandemonium." "Don't make me choose," she pleads, "I can't choose." It is only when the unrelenting doctor threatens to murder both her children that she blurts out: "Take the baby! Take my little girl."

Sophie's maddening choice was to haunt her for the rest of her life.

The terrible truth is that this piercing moment in fiction is only too accurate a description of what actually happened again and again during the holocaust. William Styron distorted the historical record by making the victim of the Nazi's fiendish cruelty a Polish Christian. In real life it was Jewish mothers who were confronted by such blasphemous choices.

(We might also note in passing that in his book Styron does not have any admirable Jewish characters. His good people are all non-Jews.)

Despite what the Nazis did to corrupt the human power to choose, the fact is that this very capacity to make significant choices is one of our most distinctive human endowments.

The word "intelligence" is derived from two Latin words—"inter" and "legere." "Inter" means between, and "legere" means to choose. Intelligence is the capacity to choose between alternative courses of actions, to make moral decisions.

Translated into theological terms this means that you and I possess freedom of will. This doctrine, which is at the very center of Jewish teaching, has had to fight off formidable opponents throughout history down to our own times.

The pagan religions of antiquity taught that man was forever doomed because he slew some deity. Hinduism viewed man as chained to Karma, the wheel of fate. In Islam man is controlled by Kismet.

When the Israelis were withdrawing from the Sinai, one of the Bedouins, who had lived under Israeli rule since 1967, expressed amazement at the value Israel placed on human life. "I don't understand why you take it so seriously when someone gets ill. Why do you get so excited? It comes from Allah."

In our own society there are many voices which strenuously deny that we are indeed free to make significant choices. Some declare that we are the products of our heredity, others affirm that our environment makes us what we are. You and I may delude ourselves into believing that we have freedom of will to choose our way, but in fact the true determinants of our destiny are beyond our power to control. We are mere puppets being manipulated by a fate not of our own making.

It was this type of thinking that prompted one 24-year-old man to sue his parents for $350,000 for what he called "psychological malparenting." He felt that they had messed up his life beyond repair. All his failures were all their fault. He was the helpless victim of their mistakes.

This evasion of responsibility for one's own life would find no support in Judaism. Rather, it would remind us that we do indeed have choices and that we create our own world by the choices we make.

Interestingly, the newest teachings of psychiatry endorse this view. While they do not deny the enormous influence of many factors we cannot control, they remind us that there is a decisive area where our own free will can enable us to take charge of our lives.

A cartoon, appearing in one of our national magazines, points in this direction. It shows a lawyer talking to his client. The caption reads: "We can't blame your problem on television. I polled the jury, and they all watch the same shows you do."

The glory and the anguish of being human derive from our ability to choose and direct the course of our lives. It is often tempting to throw up our hands and plead helplessness. But that strategy leads only to defeat and failure. Significant living is always characterized by a feeling that human will and determination play a decisive role in shaping human destiny.

Thus, *Living With Loss* by Ramsay and Noorbergen concludes with this sentence: "Ultimately whether grief destroys you or strengthens you is something only you can decide."

Most eloquent testimony of the power of the human will is provided by Dr. Victor Frankl. He wrote, "We who have lived in concentration camps can remember the men who walked through the huts comforting others, giving away their last piece of bread. They may have been few in number but they offer sufficient proof that everything can be taken from man but one thing: the last of the human freedoms—to choose one's attitude in any given set of circumstances—to choose one's own way."

Long, long ago the Torah in this week's portion put the challenge to us most directly. "Behold, I have set before you this day the blessing and the curse, life and death. And you shall choose life."

Accessories Before the Fact

—※—

A STRANGE and mysterious ritual is described in this *Sidrah*. Even the ancient Rabbis had trouble understanding it.

The Torah says: If a person is found murdered in an open field and the perpetrator of the crime is unknown, the leaders of the nearest city are obliged to offer a sacrifice of expiation. In addition, all the elders of that city are expected to wash their hands and to make the following public declaration: "Our hands have not shed this blood neither have our eyes seen it" (Deut. 21:1-9).

The Rabbis in the Talmud asked the obvious question: Why did the most respected and most honorable members of the community have to make this declaration of innocence? Who accused them of the crime? Indeed, who would even suspect them of such a terrible deed?

The Rabbis gave the following answer to their own questions: What the elders were saying in their public declaration was not a denial of outright murder. They were denying any contributory negligence on their part. "The victim did not come to us hungry and we sent him away without food; he did not come to us alone and we offered him no protection."

A penetrating and disquieting truth leaps at us from these words. The elders were obliged to assure all the people that they had not failed to do anything that might have prevented the tragedy. For if things were otherwise, if in fact they had been able to prevent the crime and had not done so, then they would have indeed been implicated and culpable.

The lesson of all this is clear. We are each morally responsible for every wrong we have the power to prevent and fail to prevent.

In our American legal system there is a category of crime known as "accessories after the fact." This includes people who aid a criminal to conceal the crime or evade capture. What Judaism is telling us is that there is another category, accessories *before* the fact. This includes people, decent people, law-abiding people, people as respectable as the elders of whom the Torah talks, who by their negligence or indifference enable preventable disasters to happen.

As Jews living in this post-Holocaust era, we are especially sensitive to the heavy burden of moral responsibility that lies on the shoulders of all those who could have done so much to help Hitler's victims and failed to do so. The voices of world religious leaders which were not raised in screaming protest, the death factories that were not bombed out of existence, the escape routes from hell that were not opened—all these are shameful monuments to moral indifference in the face of lurking disaster. How many world leaders of that dreadful era are entitled to wash their hands and say: "Our hands have not shed this blood neither have our eyes seen it"?

John F. Kennedy was fond of quoting Dante to the effect that the hottest places in hell are reserved for those who in a time of great moral crisis maintain their neutrality.

Edmund Burke pointed to the contribution that accessories before the fact make to the preventable disasters that afflict us. "All that is necessary for evil to triumph," he wrote, "is for good men to do nothing."

How about us? Have we ourselves learned anything from the tragedy of the Holocaust? Have we become more sensitive to the need to fight bigotry, hunger, disease, the threat of nuclear disaster? Have we become more committed to work for the security of Israel, the freedom of Russian Jewry, the strengthening of Judaism? Are we among the good people who do nothing?

There is a new bumper sticker which contains no words at all. It is totally blank. It is meant for those who don't want to get involved. Was this bumper sticker designed for us?

Pastor Martin Niemoller was one of the leading Protestant clergymen in Germany during the Nazi era. After the defeat of Nazism he wrote some memorable words which should serve as an effective antidote wherever we are tempted not to get involved.

"In Germany, the Nazis first came for the communists and I didn't speak up because I was not a communist.

Then they came for the Jews, and I did not speak up because I was not a Jew.

Then they came for the Trade Unionists and I didn't speak up because I was not a Trade Unionist.

Then they came for the Catholics, and I was a Protestant so I didn't speak up.

Then they came for ME . . . by that time there was no one to speak up for anyone.

To make sure this doesn't happen again, injustice to anyone, anywhere must be the concern of everyone, everywhere."

Niemoller's words are a poignant reminder that whether we like it or not we are indeed involved. Our choice is whether we do something about it or not. Our own future, the future of our children and grandchildren, depend upon our ability to choose wisely.

The Primary Law of Life

MARK TWAIN, in a characteristic mood of irreverence, once declared that what troubled him about the Bible was not the passages he did not understand but rather those he did understand. Any earnest student of the Bible can sympathize with Twain's sentiments. A case in point is found in this *Sidrah*:

"If a man has a disloyal and defiant son, who does not heed his father or mother and does not obey them even after they discipline him, his father and mother shall take hold of him and bring him out to the elders of his town at the public place of his community. They shall say to the elders of his town, 'This son of ours is disloyal and defiant; he does not heed us. He is a wastrel and a drunkard.' Thereupon the men of his town shall stone him to death. Thus you will sweep out evil from your midst; all Israel will hear and be afraid" (Deut. 21:18-21).

I'm quite sure that if this Biblical law were put as a referendum on the ballot of any community of our country it would not garner too many votes. It does grave violence to our standards of justice and equity. It certainly torpedoes our image of the caring and loving Jewish family.

It falls far below the call to compassion and mercy which the Bible itself sounds repeatedly. What, if anything, can be said in defense of this harsh piece of Biblical legislation?

First, we must look upon this law not against the background of our time but against the background of the time in which the law was promulgated. Seen in the legal context of Biblical times, the law actually represented a significant moral advance over the prevailing authority of the father in other legal systems.

In ancient times, the father's power over his children was absolute. Even later Roman law contained the "patria potestas" which gave the father the power of capital punishment over every member of his household. But see what the Torah did to limit his power. First, the father could not denounce his son by himself. "His father and mother shall take hold of him." The mother must apparently agree with the father and accompany him in pressing charges before "the elders of the town."

The introduction of "the elders of the town" into the process also seems to suggest that the charges of the father required some measure of communal validation before the stoning could take place. Moreover, by requiring the "men of the town" to do the stoning and thus taking the punishment out of the father's domain a further limitation was imposed upon the father's power.

Yet after we recognize that the Torah's law represented a significant ethical advance over the law which prevailed elsewhere in ancient times, we cannot but find our own ethical sensitivities offended by the Biblical endorsement of the father's power to inflict the ultimate punishment upon his son for being disloyal or defiant.

It might therefore be of some measure of solace to us to learn that our Talmudic Sages were apparently as unhappy with the Biblical law of the defiant son as we are. They, therefore, proceeded to impose so many conditions before the law could be invoked that it simply became impossible to practice it.

For example, the passage which we have translated above as "he does not heed us," is more literally rendered, "he does not listen to our voice." We would have expected the Torah to use the word "voices," plural, since father and mother are both registering the complaint. Since the Torah used the singular, "voice," the Sages derived from this that the only time the defiant son can be put to death was when both father and mother have *identical* voices. Well, we know how altogether unlikely it is for the male and female voices to sound precisely alike. And in the absence of this condition, the Biblical law did not apply.

When the Talmudic Sages finished working on this law they could say with truth, "There never has been a 'disloyal and defiant son' and there never will be. Why then was the law written? So that one may study it and receive reward [for performing the *mitzvah* of studying Torah]" (Sanhedrin 71a).

One of the important incidental lessons we learn from this entire discussion is that Biblical law underwent growth and development in subsequent centuries. There were also instances when the Talmudic teachers actually abrogated Biblical laws. Approximately 160 times we find in the Talmud this statement: "Originally the ruling was thus but subsequently it was changed to thus."

The Sages were ever responsive to new social, economic, and religious conditions and circumstances, or new ethical insights which required adjusting the Halakhah. If the Torah, the Written Law, were to remain vital and operative it required an Oral Law, hence the Talmud. So crucial was this ongoing process of adaptation and reinterpretation that the Sages declared that the covenant which God made with Israel was made only for the sake of the Oral Law (Gittin 60b).

Joseph Albo in his famous *Book of Roots* (1425), which is a treatise on the Jewish articles of faith, provided his rationale for the need for continuous development of Halakhah, Jewish law. "The Torah cannot be so comprehensive as to be adequate for all times, because the ever new details of human relations, their customs, and their acts are too numerous to be embraced in a book. Therefore, Moses was given orally certain general principles, only briefly alluded to in the Torah, by means of which the wise men in every generation may work out the details as they appear" (Vol. 3, Ch. 23).

Whatever justification was invoked, the towering fact remains that Jewish law is best captured not by a still photograph but by a moving picture. It was always in a vigorous state of motion. Those who would congeal it or put it into a deep-freeze render no service either to the law or to the people whose lives it was designed to regulate.

The Torah is referred to in our prayers as "a tree of life." Thus it was always alive, and change is the primary law of life. The Torah also gives life. That function it performs best when it enables its adherents to experience life in all its fullness and beauty by being true to the noblest impulses that stir them.

Ḥutzpah!

"ḤUTZPAH" IS a Hebrew word which is easier to illustrate than to translate. An oft-repeated example of *Hutzpah* is the fellow who murders his father and his mother and then pleads for mercy on the grounds that he is an orphan.

A Biblical illustration of *Hutzpah* is provided by none other than the patriarch Abraham. When he learns that the Almighty is about to destroy the cities of Sodom and Gomorrah he dares to challenge God Himself. "How can You do such a thing," he asks, "to slay the innocent as well as the guilty. . . . Shall not the Judge of all the earth deal justly?"

Another illustration of *Hutzpah* is found in the prophetic portion of this Shabbat. The author of this passage is the Prophet Isaiah who is believed to have lived in Babylon during the exile in the sixth century B.C.E. His audience is a despondent people which has despaired of ever being restored to its homeland.

It is to such a people at such a dark time that the prophet has the *Hutzpah*, the bold audacity, to offer some incredible promises. The people will indeed be restored to the land from which it was exiled. Moreover, "Nations shall walk by your light; kings, by your shining radiance" (Is. 60:3).

Here is a miserable remnant of a once proud people, uprooted from its land, stripped of its sovereignty, bereft of all hope. For this battered people the prophet dares to foretell a glorious future.

Unlike every other people for whom exile meant disappearance, the Jewish people will experience the miracle of return and rebirth. And rebirth will be followed by a spiritual renaissance so brilliant that its incandescence will illuminate the paths for the other nations as well. They too will walk by the light that Israel will generate, kings will be guided by Israel's luminous radiance.

Now the astonishing thing about the prophet's audacious promises is that they came true. Israel was restored. Israel has been a light unto the nations.

At a time when inside the U.N. and within many nations there is a concerted effort to blacken the name of the Jew, it might be helpful to listen to some of mankind's most respected voices appraising the true role of our people in history.

The Russian writer, Maxim Gorky, wrote: "I believe that Jewish wisdom is more all-human and universal than any other; and this not only because of its immemorial age, not only because it is the first born, but also because of the powerful humanness that saturates it, because of its high estimate of man."

The celebrated novelist Pearl Buck reflected on the role of our people in the various countries where we have lived. "I have never seen a country," she wrote, "or a culture which was not the better for having the contribution of the Jewish people."

In his *Literature and Dogma*, Matthew Arnold wrote: "As long as the world lasts, all who want to make progress in righteousness will come to Israel for inspiration as the people who have the sense for righteousness most glowing and strongest."

Ellsworth Huntington in his *Pulse of Progress* was most effusive in his praise of our people: "The Jews are probably the greatest of all peoples. Has any other people so persistently produced an almost ceaseless string of great men for three or four thousand years?"

And the Christian clergyman and editor Lyman Abbott wrote: "When sometimes our own unchristian prejudices flame out against the Jewish people, let us remember that all that we have and all that we are we owe, under God, to what Judaism has given us."

Isaiah's audacious promise that nations would walk by the bright lights our people would kindle, has indeed been fulfilled. Among other things he taught us that we often need a massive dose of *Hutzpah* to dream a mighty dream, and then we have to marshal the strength to make the dream come true.

Where Is God
When Tragedy Strikes?

QUESTION: In the newspaper account of the funeral service for a twenty-year-old murder victim, the officiating rabbi is quoted as offering the following prayer: "Eternal God, our Creator, who makes and takes, You have given, now You have taken away. May she rest in peace." Is the prayer that the rabbi offered a standard Jewish prayer, or was he expressing his own sentiments? Do you agree with those sentiments?

ANSWER: The prayer that the rabbi offered was not a standard Jewish prayer. It is, however, based on the well-known verse which Job uttered in the face of his multiple tragedies. "The Lord has given, and the Lord has taken away; blessed be the name of the Lord" (Job 1:21). This verse is included in the traditional Jewish funeral service, and I am sure that many rabbis read it.

The officiating rabbi whom you quote paraphrased the words of Job in the prayer he offered at a desperately difficult time both for the family and for the rabbi.

I empathize deeply with his effort to console a devastated family, but I confess that I am uncomfortable with his choice of words. They seem to imply that it was God who has "taken away" the twenty-year-old innocent victim, that the murder of the young woman was God's doing or God's will. I find that idea totally unacceptable.

Our belief in God affirms the sacredness of life and the sanctity of every human being, created in His image. The Author of life urges us to care for life, to treasure it, to preserve it. Therefore, it is inconceivable that God would send a madman to destroy a promising young life and thereby, incidentally, inflict on her parents in this instance the unspeakable horror of burying a second child.

I cannot conceive of the murderer as God's messenger. On the contrary, everything this murderer has done is in flagrant violation of God's will.

God has endowed each of us with the freedom to choose how we shall live. We may either do His will or flaunt it. He says to us: "Behold, I have put before you life and death, blessing and curse. Choose life—if you and your offspring would live—by loving the Lord, your God, heeding His commands and holding fast to Him" (Deut. 30:19-20).

Though He pleads with us to choose life, we can choose not to choose life. When we spurn life and choose death, when we pervert justice and do injustice, when we resort to violence, corruption, greed, selfishness, oppression—when we do any of these things, the responsibility rests with us. It is squarely our own and not God's. "The fault, dear Brutus, is not in our stars, but in ourselves, that we are underlings."

Where is God in this terrible tragedy?

God is in the compassion we feel for the bereaved parents.

God is in the sympathy and in the support that kind friends extend to the survivors.

God is in our resolve to apprehend the murderer and to prevent further shedding of innocent blood.

God is in the strength that the victim's loved ones will somehow find as they make their way through the valley of the shadow.

God is in the healing that will come to them ever so slowly but ever so surely.

God is in the power of the human spirit to rise above sorrow and to transmute suffering into song, adversity into artistry, and pain into poetry.

We come from God and we return to Him and with the Source of life no soul is ever lost. God is also in the great gift of remembrance. As the poet said, God gave us memory so that we might have roses in December.

Big Lesson in a Little Word

IN HEBREW there are no words consisting of a single letter. The shortest Hebrew word has two letters. But no word is so small that our Sages could not find in it a big idea.

An excellent illustration is found in a rabbinic comment on a verse in this week's *Sidrah*. When God announced to Moses the imminence of his death He says to him, *"Behold*, the time is drawing near for you to die" (Deut. 31:14).

The Biblical word, which is translated "behold," consists of two Hebrew letters, *Hay* and *Nun*, and is pronounced *Hayn*. This same word occurs in the Biblical narrative some forty years earlier when Moses is addressing the Almighty. When God charges Moses to tell the Israelites that He has seen their suffering and is about to redeem them, Moses protests: *"Behold*, they will not believe me nor listen to me for they will say the Lord did not appear to you" (Ex. 4:1). Here, too, *Hayn* is used.

The occurrence of the word *Hayn* in these two verses prompted the Sages to see a causal connection between them. Thus, the Rabbis picture the Almighty as saying to Moses: "At the moment when you said, *'Behold*, they will not believe me,' at that very moment *'Behold*, the time drew near for you to die.'" What the Sages were trying to tell us was that when Moses was riddled by self-doubt, when he had no faith in his credibility with his own people, at that point his effectiveness as a leader was gone.

If we might generalize from this rabbinic comment we could put it this way—we achieve as we believe. The decisive area of our accomplishments is located in our own mind. Thus, our Sages anticipated perhaps the insight of William James, one of the leading American pioneers in the field of psychology. "The greatest discovery of my generation," wrote James, "is that human beings can alter their lives by altering their attitudes."

Walter B. Wintle put that thought more simply in his oft-quoted poem:

"If you think you are beaten, you are;
If you think you dare not, you don't.
If you'd like to win, but think you can't
It's almost a cinch you won't.
. . . Life's battles don't always go
To the stronger or faster man;
But soon or late the man who wins
Is the one who thinks he can."

One thirteen-year-old stumbled upon this truth. A friend had sent him a book as a Bar Mitzvah present. The book was lost in transit and when the empty carton reached the lad he muttered above his disappointment. "Well, it's the thought that counts."

The boy's philosophic effort to console himself points to a lesson that is gaining increasing attention in our time. It is indeed the thought that counts. The whole school of cognitive therapy has underlined in red the decisive influence our thoughts exercise over our moods, our self-image, our achievements. If we have bad habits of thinking we create for ourselves private black holes. Our severest handicap is a distorted self-image. When we think of ourselves as unlovable, unsuccessful, incapable, we tend to become all these things. Conversely, when we have a positive self-image our achievements will reflect that self-appraisal. We tend to become what we imagine ourselves to be. Our thoughts are the controlling factor.

An athletic coach once advised his pole vault man to place on his wall a large picture of himself clearing the bar in fine form. He did this not because he wanted the young man to become conceited, but because he knew that a crucial determinant of the athlete's performance would be his feeling about what he could accomplish. The coach considered it very important that the young man have a positive image of himself. And indeed it worked in the competition because as the young fellow said: "It's the thought that counts."

So often we try very desperately to change the circumstances of our lives, to alter the external environment. We forget that the decisive arena where our destiny is determined is in the internal environment. Far more significant than the landscape for lives is the "inscape"—to use a word coined by G. K. Chesterton.

The late Golda Meir has left us an excellent illustration of what we are talking about. Here are her own words:

"I was never a beauty. There was a time when I was sorry about that, when I was old enough to understand the importance of it and, looking in any mirror, realized it was something I was never going to have. Then I found what I wanted to do in life, and being called pretty no longer had any importance.

"It was only much later that I realized that *not* being beautiful was a blessing in disguise. It forced me to develop my inner resources. I came to understand that women who cannot lean on their beauty and need to make something on their own have the advantage."

Golda Meir was not able to change her face but she was able to change the way she looked at her face. Then she discovered a greater source of beauty within herself.

We should all want to be rich, wouldn't we? We can all be rich if we follow the advice of our Sages: "Who is rich?" they asked. Their answer: "He who is content with his lot." Whether we are rich or not depends not on what we have but rather how we look upon what we have. The disgruntled person, the envious person, the greedy person is eternally poor. But the one who has learned to look upon his possessions with gratitude and awareness has thereby come into great fortune. It is indeed the thought that counts.

Perhaps this is the big lesson our Sages wanted us to learn from one little word.

The Fine Art of Forgetting

THE RABBI in Leon Uris' novel about the persecuted Jews in the Warsaw Ghetto, *Mila 18*, makes a penetrating observation. He declares that when a Jew says "I believe," he really means, "I remember." It is quite true that historical memories are the glue which has kept our people together over the centuries.

A Jew is born 4000 years old. We have a special Sabbath called *"Zakhor,"* remember. All of our festivals are designed to relive ancestral experiences in ages past. "You shall remember that you were a slave in the land of Egypt," is a Biblical exhortation that is repeated again and again.

In our personal lives there are a host of rituals designed as mnemonics to help us remember our loved ones who have died. There is the Kaddish, yahrzeit, Yizkor. We name our children and our grandchildren after them. We put their names on memorials in Synagogues, we plant trees, and we give *tzedakah* in their memory.

For all the emphasis we place on the importance of remembering, it is appropriate that we reflect from time to time on the importance of forgetting.

Ingrid Bergman once said that she was fortunate to possess the two assets on which happiness depends—good health and a poor memory. That talented lady gave us a much needed reminder that the ability to forget is no less important than the ability to remember.

We often apologize for forgetting things. In his farewell address,

Moses rebukes his people for forgetting a crucial fact: "You forgot the God who brought you forth" (Deut. 32:18).

But important as is the power to remember, no less important is the power to forget. Life, as we know it, would be unbearable if we were not blessed with what one eight-year-old called "a good forgettery."

If we had to live each day burdened with the weight of past griefs and bereavements, if we could not banish from our minds our accumulated failures, fears and frustrations, if the wounds we suffer on life's battlefield were always raw and gaping—then life would be a heavy curse.

Long ago, our Sages taught us this same truth. In a charming legend we are told that after the Almighty finished creating the world He was about to release when He suddenly realized that He had omitted an indispensable ingredient without which life could not endure. God had forgotten to include the power to forget. And so He blessed the world with that special gift, and then He was content that it was now fit for human habitation.

Many of us could use that gift. So many families remain splintered and fragmented because of some slight, real or imagined, suffered long years ago which the offended party cannot or will not forget.

Recently I was discussing funeral services for a father who was survived by two sons. When I asked the son who was making the arrangements where the family would sit *Shivah*, I was requested to make no public announcement because the sons would not sit together in one house. The reason? Their wives stopped talking to each other years ago over some invitation which was not reciprocated. At least, that's what he thought it was. By now, he was not quite sure what had caused the split in the family. He could not remember the source of the conflict, but whatever it was, neither brother could forget it.

Many a marriage could stand a healthy dose of forgetting. One man complained to his friend that whenever his wife gets angry she becomes historical. "You mean hysterical," the friend corrected him. "No," said the husband, "I mean historical. She starts listing everything I did wrong in the last 27 years."

Lewis E. Lawes, who served many years as the warden of Sing Sing, once said that our prisons are filled with people who could not or would not forget.

So many lives are cluttered with all kinds of destructive memories. They carry accumulated resentments, hurts, sorrows and disappointments suffered in the arena of life. The price for such remembering is exorbitant. It includes our emotional and mental health. When the Torah admonishes us not to "bear a grudge," it is urging us for our own sake to use our God-given power to forget.

An anonymous poet put into rhyme some thoughts about forgetting we would do well to remember:

> "This world would be for us a happier place
> And there would be less of regretting
> If we would remember to practice with grace,
> The very fine art of forgetting."

The Unreachable
Promised Land

"AND THE LORD said unto Moses: 'This is the land which I swore to Abraham, Isaac and Jacob . . . I have let you see it with your own eyes, but you shall not cross there.' So Moses the servant of the Lord died in the land of Moab, at the command of the Lord" (Deut. 34: 4–5).

Whenever I come to this passage in the Torah, I recall the sense of disappointment that filled me when, as a child, I read this Biblical story for the first time. How cruel was the sense of frustration I shared with Moses. He had dedicated his very life to a single goal which drew him irresistibly on. To achieve it, he had led his people through four perilous decades, inspiring them with courage, battling their recurrent doubts, buttressing their sagging faith, keeping steadfastly before them the vision of the ultimate destination—the Promised Land. When, at last, he stands with them on the very threshhold of fulfillment, Moses is permitted only a glimpse of the Promised Land, before death rudely intervenes to claim him.

To have struggled so long for an overarching goal only to be halted at the precise moment when it is virtually within reach—that appeared to be too depressing a climax to so noble a human adventure. It seemed to betray the very faith by which Moses himself had lived. It seemed to empty the vision which Moses had so resolutely championed.

Our Rabbis in the Midrash in their amplification of this closing chapter in the life of Moses added greater poignancy to it. They picture Moses as pleading fervently with God to permit him to enter the land, if not as a person then at least as a bird or in the form of some other animal; if not alive, then dead. But all in vain. The bitter decree is irreversible.

With maturity, however, the sense of disappointment was mellowed by the realization that in the untimely death of Moses the Bible was conveying an inescapable truth of human experience. The great always die too soon. For it is in the essence of greatness that it sets up for itself goals which are too large to be achieved in any lifetime, however long. Big people are unsatisfied with small objectives. Every Moses inevitably leaves his final Jordan uncrossed.

Dean Stanley amplified this thought when he wrote: "To labor and not see the end of our labors, to sow and not to reap, to be removed from this earthly scene before our work has been appreciated . . . is a law so common in the highest characters of history, that none can be said to be altogether exempt from its operation."

I am tempted to make the generalization that it is only small people who reach their Promised Land in their lifetime. If a man is concerned only with acquiring a new home, or a higher income bracket, or a political office, or financial security in his twilight years—he can very well reach his Promised Land. But what of the man whose Promised Land is the defeat of disease, the melting of prejudice, the triumph of democracy, the fortification of Judaism— is he likely to reach his destination? And yet who will deny that it is in the very striving after these goals that life acquires its highest significance?

Our Sages seem to have been pointing in this direction when they said that every Jew is obliged to participate in "a *Mitzvah* which is designed for the generations." They were apparently talking about goals which in their very nature defy easy attainment, dreams so large that the road to their realization must be long and arduous.

Perhaps we have here a clue to what Oscar Wilde meant in his paradoxical comment: "There are two tragedies in life. One is not getting what you want. The other is getting what you want." We should be suspicious of Promised Lands which are too easily reached. They may not be worth the journey.

"A man's reach should exceed his grasp or what's a heaven for?"

Holy Days, Festivals, and Special Occasions

Time: Ally or Adversary?

THE BEGINNING of a New Year on the Jewish calendar focuses our attention sharply on the relentless passing of time. Actually the first day of Tishre slips in as quietly as does any other day of the year.

There are no special peals of thunder or bolts of lightning to proclaim that a new year has begun. In fact, for nearly 100 percent of the people on our planet it isn't a new year at all. But whenever one's new year begins it is an occasion to reflect on the meaning of the time and how we relate to it.

Is time an ally or an adversary?

The poet Yeats wrote: "I spit in the face of time that has transfigured me." But Benjamin Franklin kept on his desk two boxes. One box was marked: "Problems it will take time to solve." The other, "Problems time has already solved." For Yeats time was an enemy, for Franklin a friend.

Time is neither. It is neutral. It is what we do with time that matters.

Will Rogers once told about a druggist who was asked if he ever took time off to have a good time. The druggist said, no, he didn't, but he sold a lot of headache medicine to those who did.

One thing we can say with certainty. Time moves steadily ahead. Like manna, it cannot be hoarded. Nor can it be reversed. The film of life cannot be rewound. Nor can it be halted in its flight. Sometimes we come to a moment so exquisite that we understand the poet's plea: "O moment stay, thou art fair."

But we cannot stop time in its tracks.

What can we do with time? Many things. We can kill it, we can waste it, we can use it, we can invest it.

Prisoners serve time; musicians mark time; idlers pass time; speeding motorists make time; referees call time; historians record time; scorekeepers keep time.

Each day every one of us is given the identical amount of a fresh supply of time—24 hours of 60 minutes each. This is the only time we have—not a year, not a month, not a week. The moment pressing against us now, this day, is ours to use. Once it is gone it is irretrievable.

Horace Mann once put this announcement in a newspaper's lost and found column: "Lost somewhere between sunrise and sunset, two golden hours, each set with 60 diamond minutes. No reward is offered, for they are gone forever." Like money, time has a way of slipping through our fingers with nothing to show for it.

Often we complain about the speed with which time passes. We shouldn't. If last year passed quickly, it is an indication that it was a good year for us.

Last year did not hurry by for all. For those who lost a dear one, the time of mourning did not pass quickly. For those who paced hospital corridors, who waited for a loved one's return, who searched in vain for a job—for them time did not fly by. At a time of loneliness, grief, anguish, worry, a single night can be an endless eternity.

At whatever speed last year moved, it is gone. No, it is here forever, woven into the very texture of our lives.

What shall we do with the year we have just begun? Professor Abraham Joshua Heschel left us an important clue when he wrote: "Judaism is a religion of time, aiming at the sanctification of time."

Yes, we can sanctify time. Not only is Rosh Hashanah a holy day, and Yom Kippur and Shabbat, but every day is holy if we choose to sanctify it. Remember the weekday to keep it holy.

How does time become holy? It becomes holy when a part of it is given to others, when we share and care and listen. Time is sanctified when we use it—

to forgive and ask forgiveness;
to remember things too long forgotten and to forget things too long remembered;

to reclaim sacred things too casually abandoned and to abandon shabby things too highly cherished;

to remember that life's most crucial question is—how are we using time?

Yes, time flies but we are the navigators. More important than counting time is making time count.

As we face the new year there is a special urgency to the prayer of the Psalmist: "Teach us to number our days so that we may attain a heart of wisdom."

What Do You See?

THE BIBLICAL INCIDENT which figures most prominently in the Rosh Hashanah service is the story of the *Akedah*, the binding of Isaac. We encounter a host of references to this towering episode throughout the liturgy of this day.

Our Sages tell us that as Abraham and Isaac and their servants approached Mount Moriah, the divinely designated summit for the sacrifice, Abraham turned to his servants with a question: "Do you see anything in the distance?" They stared and shook their heads. "No, we see only the trackless wastes of the wilderness." Abraham then turned to Isaac with the very same question. "Yes," said the son, "I see a mountain, majestic and beautiful, and a cloud of glory hovers above it." It was at this point that Abraham directed his servants to remain behind while he and Isaac continued alone.

Here then are two people facing in the same direction, surveying the identical scene, coming up with completely different impressions. One sees only emptiness and barrenness ahead. The second sees the majestic and challenging mountains. The difference obviously lay in the eyes of the beholder.

Skipping the centuries now and coming right down to where we are, let us each ask ourselves the question—"What do you see?" As we shall soon realize, this can be a decisive question.

On these days when we pray for life, we might, therefore, ask ourselves—what do you see in life?

When you look at your life, do you always see reasons for grumbling or gratefulness? Do you feel that you have been shortchanged or overpaid? Do you constantly feel your cup is half empty, or in the words of the psalmist, "my cup runneth over"?

Matthew Arnold has written that "one thing only has been lent to youth and age in common—it is discontent." Our favorite posture is one of protest and we who have so much, so very, very much, often permit the one thing we lack to blind us to the wealth we possess.

Another question. When you look at life, do you see only your life and your needs, or do you see the lives and the needs of others as well? Do you see life as a campaign of acquisition or as an adventure in sharing? This question is basic because it spills over into every area of life. How do you regard your job or profession? Is it only a means of providing you and your family with your needs and luxuries, or is it also an opportunity to render a service? How do you regard your mate in marriage? Someone created for your comfort and convenience or someone whose life you can enrich and enlarge? How do you regard your fellow human being? One whose main function in life is to serve as a stepping-stone to your success or someone with hopes and needs just like yourself?

One more question. When you look at life, do you look at it with fear or with faith?

It is impossible, of course, to be entirely free of fear. There is literally no one without his share of fears and apprehensions. The bravest of people have a fear of losing loved ones, a fear of losing health and fortune. To a certain extent, our fears are the saving of us. The man who fears failure develops his skills and his talents more fully. The fear of separation from loved ones spurs us on in medical and scientific research, and "the beginning of wisdom," the psalmist tells us, "is fear of the Lord." But fear becomes a matter of deep concern when it becomes exaggerated and morbid.

The cardinal irreverence in Judaism is to be afraid of life, for when we fear life we betray a lack of faith in God. Faith in God does not mean to believe that sorrow will never invade our homes, or illness never strike us and our loved ones. To believe in God is to have faith that He will give us, amidst all vicissitudes, the strength to endure, and the power to hold on and see it through, the capacity to translate even our trials and our tribulations into moral and spiritual victories.

What do you see?

The Four R's of Repentance

THE OPENING WORD of this Sabbath's prophetic portion is *Shuvah* which means "return." This word gives this Sabbath its special name—*Shabbat Shuvah*—the Sabbath of Return. The Shabbat between Rosh Hashanah and Yom Kippur, when this prophetic portion is read, occurs during the Ten Days of Penitence and the dominant theme of this holy season is captured in the words of the prophet Hosea: "Return, O Israel, to the Lord your God . . ." (Hosea 14:2).

On the Jewish calendar, this is the time for introspection, self-evaluation, self-examination.

The mood of these days is contrite and sober. How could it be otherwise when we focus the spotlight of conscience upon ourselves? Moral inventory, honestly taken, is rarely conducive to heightened self-appreciation.

The gulf between what we could be and what we are, between our vast potentialities and our limited achievements, underscores the need for repentance—a return to God, an upreaching for the Highest. However, the awareness of our sins and our human frailty is relieved by the comforting faith that we can conquer sin. We need not remain the unwilling captives of our transgressions. Given a determined will on our part, we can count on divine assistance to liberate us from the shackles of our own fashioning.

Thus our Sages taught: "If a man opens his heart even as slightly as a needle's eye, God will open it as wide as the gateway to the Temple hall." God is not only our judge but also our ally in the struggle for moral regeneration.

How do we earn God's forgiveness? The discipline of repentance consists of three distinct steps.

Initially, there must be the conscious awareness of having sinned. This is more easily said than accomplished. The very word sin is today suspect. We make mistakes, we use bad judgment, we are misled—but we don't sin anymore. Sin is old-fashioned. It has gone out of style—at least the word has. But unless we acknowledge the awesome reality of sin in our lives, the very notion of repentance is ludicrous.

To admit that it is we who have sinned means to avoid the temptation to blame our environment, our mates, our circumstances, our society, our emotional conditioning. We have picked up enough of the jargon of the psychiatrist to provide escape hatches from feelings of guilt. As children we may have felt unwanted or unloved. Our parents malparented. We were subject to frustration. We are bundles of complexes, reflexes, fixations over which we have no control.

Like the teenage gangs in "West Side Story" we have our ready-made explanation for any dereliction:

> "Dear, kindly Sergeant Krupke
> You gotta understand.
> It's just our bringing upke
> That gets us outa hand.
> Our mothers are all junkies,
> Our fathers are all drunks.
> Golly, Moses, naturally we're punks."

The first requirement for repentance is to resist rationalization, projection and the other mental masks we use to disguise our moral failures. We need first the courage to accuse ourselves.

The consciousness of sin must be followed by its confession directly to God without benefit of human mediator. Judaism does not empower its clergy to forgive sin. Only God has that power.

Many of us are aware of the prominent role the confession of sins occupies in the Yom Kippur liturgy. The "*Al Het*" is recited no fewer than five times. But the confession of sins is not confined to Yom Kippur. The daily *Amidah* which we recite three times each weekday contains the prayer: "Forgive us, our Father, for we have sinned;

pardon us, our King, for we have transgressed. . . ." And it is appropriate at this point in the silent prayer to add any specific sin which weighs on our hearts.

Having confessed our sins, we must resolve not to repeat the sin. Remorse without resolution is inadequate.

"How do we know," asked Rebbe Bunim, "that our sin has been forgiven?" He answered his own question. "When we have another opportunity to commit that sin and we resist it, then we know that we are free of that sin." True atonement involves amendment.

This then is the three-fold spiritual strategy to rid ourselves of sin—recognition, recitation, renunciation.

Where the sin is against a fellow-man, a fourth step is required—reparation.

"For transgressions between a human being and God, repentance on Yom Kippur brings atonement. For transgressions between one human being and another, Yom Kippur brings no atonement until the injured party is reconciled" (Mishnah, Yomah 8:9).

Morris Joseph accurately reflected Jewish teaching when he wrote: "We may be truly sorry for our shortcomings, sincere in our entreaties for pardon, earnest in our desire for reconciliation with the Highest, but unless, to crown all this, we solemnly resolve to make a better fight for Duty henceforth the Day of Atonement will have done little for us."

Thus, this sacred season summons us not only to return to God; it summons us also to return to one another. In harmony with the Highest and in fellowship with each other we venture forth into the New Year morally cleansed and spiritually renewed.

On Becoming Whole

SYNAGOGUES ARE more crowded on this day than on any other day of the year. Yom Kippur, the Day of Atonement, is a day of prayer, fasting and self-evaluation.

A prominent feature of the spiritual landscape of the day is the confessional—the recitation of the sins that we have committed, that fill us with remorse, and for which we ask a merciful God to forgive us. One of those sins is worth pondering.

"The sin we have sinned before You with the confession of our mouths." We have confessed great truths with our mouths but we have not translated them into deeds. This is the sin of lip service, words that become not a stimulus to action but a substitute for them. It happens to be one of our most prevalent sins, too.

Ninety-five percent of the American people answered "yes" to a survey question: "Do you believe in God?" Another question in the same survey read: "Would you say your religious beliefs have any effect on your practice in business or politics?" To this question a majority answered "no." Their religious beliefs did not influence their daily conduct. For too many of us religion has become respectable but irrelevant.

"The sin we have sinned before You with the confession of our mouths."

There is too often a yawning chasm between our affirmations and our actions, between our principles and our practices, between our conscience and our conduct, between our creeds and our deeds.

There are massive contradictions and hypocrisies which stain our lives. Who can estimate how much they contribute to our emotional ailments? We are split spiritual personalities.

We swear allegiance to one set of principles and live by another.

We extol self-control and practice self-indulgence.

We proclaim brotherhood and harbor prejudice.

We laud character but strive to climb to the top at any cost.

We erect houses of worship but our shrines are our places of business and recreation.

We are "proud" to be Jews but make too little effort to live out our Jewishness.

We talk one way and live another.

We embrace lofty ideals and then demean them by shabby acts.

We are suffering from a distressing cleavage between the truths we affirm and the values we live by. Our souls are the battlegrounds for civil wars while we try to live serene lives in houses divided against themselves.

The integrity which is so indispensable to vital and creative living is thus denied us. We are fragmented and fractured when we yearn to be intact and whole.

It was Harold Laski who warned that "the surest way to bring about the destruction of a civilization is to allow the abyss to widen between the values men praise and the values they permit to operate." We overlook this warning at our own peril.

One of the crucial functions that Yom Kippur performs for us is to sensitize us to the inconsistencies in our lives. It also urges us not to grow reconciled to them, not to accept them as either inevitable or final. For it is so tempting (and so natural?) to cease struggling, to surrender, to come to terms with our internal fractures. We tend to wink at our hypocrisies, we cease to be disturbed over the moral cleavages which should agitate us profoundly.

We too often resemble the patron at the bar who upon finishing his scotch and soda hurled the empty glass against the mirrored wall that faced him. When the bartender expressed his surprise and dismay, the man apologized profusely. He was genuinely sorry but he simply couldn't help himself. Every time he had a drink he had this uncontrollable urge to smash the glass against the wall. "Then I always feel guilty."

The bartender sympathized with the contrite drinker and urged him to see a psychiatrist. The patron assured him that he would do so.

Several months later he returned to the bar, ordered his scotch and soda and, as before, smashed the empty glass against the wall.

"I thought you were going to see a psychiatrist," exclaimed the bartender. "I did," boasted the patron, "and he did me a world of good. Now I no longer feel guilty."

Yom Kippur has for its prime purpose the shattering of our complacency. It urges us to narrow, if not altogether to bridge, the abyss between our professions and our practice, between the "confession of our mouths" and the works of our hands, hearts and minds. It summons us to restore our battered integrity.

The biographer of D. H. Lawrence made a profound observation which was prompted by his study of his bitterly disappointed subject and which goes to the very heart of this matter. "When a man is sure that all he wants is happiness," writes Middleton Murry, "then most grievously he deceives himself. All men desire happiness but they want something different, compared to which happiness is trivial, and in the absence of which happiness turns to dust and ashes in the mouth. There are many names for that which men need but the simplest is wholeness."

Yom Kippur asks us to become whole.

Guilt—Guardian of
Our Goodness

A FEW YEARS AGO the late Dore Schary, a strongly committed Jew, was asked if he would compose a prayer for the new High Holy Day Prayer Book, *Mahzor Hadash*. He graciously consented and after some time he submitted a sensitive and moving piece called "Not Guilty?". Instinctively, he focused on the themes of guilt and repentance which are at the very heart of the holiest season of the Jewish calendar.

On Yom Kippur we pray for forgiveness and, of course, there can be no forgiveness without a prior awareness of having done wrong, a sense of guilt for having done wrong, and a profound yearning to remove the guilt through genuine remorse for the past and a resolve not to repeat the wrongs which produced the feeling of guilt.

Even as we speak about guilt we know that we sound very old-fashioned. The guilt feeling has had its legitimacy questioned in recent years. Somewhere along the line it has gotten itself a bad name. It is regarded as the stuff that other people lay on us. It's a bad trip to be avoided at all cost.

According to some novelists and comedians one of the heaviest traffickers in guilt is that much maligned character—the Jewish mother. One stand-up Jewish comedian brings down the house with the one-liner: "My mother is the east coast distributor for guilt."

One syndicated columnist wrote recently: "Guilt is a pollutant and we don't need any more of it in the world."

Dr. Theodore Rubin, a psychiatrist, calls guilt "a destructive form of self-hate."

A whole spate of recent books and articles have as their theme: "Stop Feeling So Guilty." Our cartoon friend Ziggy accurately reflects the prevailing attitude toward guilt. He is lying on the couch and says to his analyst: "Lately I've been feeling guilty about my guilt feelings."

To be sure there is indeed a great deal of unmerited guilt, neurotic guilt, unearned guilt that do terrible things to undeserving people.

One desolate mother punished herself mercilessly over the death of her daughter 15 years earlier, because she had encouraged her to undergo the surgery which proved fatal. That two physicians had encouraged the surgery hardly entered into her misery-producing feelings.

Another woman, a Holocaust survivor, can not forgive herself for surviving the fiery ordeal which consumed her parents, husband and three brothers. That she did not contribute in the slightest to their deaths has done nothing to mitigate her self-flagellation.

And what of the guilt that unjustifiably consumes so many parents when their children don't turn out the way they had hoped. "Where did I go wrong?" they ask self-accusingly, as though any parent is omnipotent and has total control in determining the course of a child's life.

Conscience is a great servant but a terrible master. It is somewhat like an automobile horn. It is useful for warding off impending danger. But if a horn gets stuck it's a terrible nuisance.

However, because guilt can be neurotic and unearned, it does not mean that all guilt is suspect. Certain acts (including perhaps the attempt to abolish guilt) should indeed produce guilt feelings. Cheating, lying, stealing, breaking promises, malicious gossip, failing to honor commitments, indifference to suffering, insensitivity to others' feelings, failure to expand our horizons and deepen our sympathies—shouldn't these things produce within us at this holy season a profound sense of spiritual discomfort? And if we do not feel guilt for such sins haven't we already suffered the greatest of all punishments—a coarsening of the fabric of our lives, an abdication of all that makes us human?

Dr. Willard Paylin, a psychiatrist, calls guilt "a guardian of our goodness. . . . It represents the noblest and most painful of all struggles."

Another psychoanalyst, Dr. Allen Wheelis, called guilt "the socializing emotion." He added: "I don't think we can have a civilization without it. Guilt feelings do not have to mean the presence of a neurosis. They more likely mean the presence of a soul. And when we do wrong we should feel guilty. . . . A sense of guilt may be uncomfortable to have but it is fatal to be without."

The late Dr. Abraham Joshua Heschel put the matter in his inimitable lyric words: "The cure of the soul begins with a sense of embarrassment, embarrassment at our pettiness, prejudices, envy and conceit, embarrassment at the profanation of life." Only as we feel this embarrassment, this guilt, can we hope to strive for the forgiveness to which this holy season summons us. Then we can say as Dore Schary did at the end of his prayer:

> "And I am now repentant
> And will repair what damage I have done,
> Repay the debts I owe,
> And pray to wipe the word "Guilty" from the book,
> And ask again this year
> That my name be inscribed in the Book of Life.
> Then, when next year the list is read again,
> Perhaps somewhere—some one place, at least—
> I can say '*not guilty*'—no repentance due."

When God Measures Us

THE FESTIVAL OF SUKKOT, is distinguished first by the *Sukkah*, the temporary booth, which almost every synagogue and many a Jewish family erects.

Sukkot is further distinguished by the use of the palm and citron, the *Lulav* and *Etrog*, which are carried in joyous processions around the synagogue at morning services of the Festival. This we do in accordance with the injunction of the Torah: "And you shall take . . . the fruit of goodly trees, branches of palm trees, the boughs of thick trees, and willows of the brook, and you shall rejoice before the Lord your God seven days" (Lev. 23:40).

Of all the four species of plants here mentioned, it is "the fruit of the goodly tree," the *Etrog*, which receives the most attention. It has beauty and aroma and special care is taken to select an especially attractive one. Why so much fuss over the *Etrog*?

The *Etrog*, say the Jewish moralists, is shaped like the human heart, and the most important part of the human being is the heart, the source of compassion, kindness and generosity.

When Nellie Sachs, the German Jewish poetess was awarded the Nobel Prize for literature, her citation said in part: "She invoked in her poetry the sound at the heart of the world."

When God measures a human being, we are told, He puts the tape around the heart not the head. The human heart that responds to the sound at the heart of the world is the truest index of a person's humanity.

There is a desperate shortage of kindness in the world.

So many of us starve for it most of the time. One doctor said recently that ninety percent of all mental illness which he has treated could have been prevented or cured by ordinary kindness. What an indictment against us! If we see a hungry man, who is so callous that he will not give him a piece of bread? But all around us people are starving and we do not have the time or the thoughtfulness or the compassion to speak a kind word, perform a gracious act, make a call, drop a line, to give bread to emaciated spirits.

Civilization, it has been said, is just a slow process in learning to be kind. The man who has not learned that lesson remains uneducated regardless of the number of diplomas on his office walls or the number of degrees that follow his signature. The man who has learned to be kind has mastered the most vital subject in life's curriculum. His formal schooling may have been meager, his familiarity with books not very intimate. If he has learned how to bring a ray of light where there is darkness, a word of cheer where spirits have been crushed by circumstances—that man is civilized. "The All Merciful desires the heart" is the way our tradition tells us.

Dr. Haim Ginnott, the late psychiatrist and author, quotes in his *Teacher and Child* a note which a principal sent to all his teachers on the first day of school.

"Dear Teacher:

I am a survivor of a concentration camp. My eyes saw what no man should witness.

Gas chambers built by learned engineers.

Children poisoned by educated physicians.

Infants killed by trained nurses.

Women and babies shot and burned by high school and college graduates.

So, I am suspicious of education.

My request is: Help your students become human. Your efforts must never produce learned monsters, skilled psychopaths, educated Eichmanns.

Reading, writing, arithmetic are important only if they serve to make our children more humane."

In our time, more than ever before, what will count most will not be the lessons we learn by heart but the lessons the heart will learn.

Much Obliged

SUKKOT IS ALSO known in the Torah as the Festival of Ingathering, celebrating the autumn harvest: "When you have gathered in the yield of the land, you shall observe the festival of the Lord . . ." (Lev. 23:39).

It was this dimension of the festival which guided the pilgrims in 1621 to set aside a day of thanksgiving when they gathered in their harvests after their first harsh year in the New World.

Anyone at all familiar with the Jewish tradition knows that the mood of thanksgiving is not confined to Sukkot.

The obligation to cultivate a lively sense of appreciation for the manifold blessings a gracious God heaps upon us daily, runs like a golden thread throughout the fabric of our religious faith. The Jew who adheres faithfully to his spiritual obligations is enjoined to recite no less than one hundred blessings from the time he awakes in the morning to the time he retires at night.

So highly did our Sages prize the mood of thanksgiving that one of them declared: "In the time to come, all the offerings will be abolished except the thank-offering; all the prayers will be abolished except the prayers of thanksgiving." Thus the art of giving thanks enjoyed special pre-eminence over all other religious disciplines.

And yet, as we view human nature at work, we cannot fail to be impressed with the difficulty so many of us have in developing the art of giving thanks.

Our gripes and grumblings are louder than our expressions of gratitude. We complain more often than we experience contentment. Our awareness of what we lack is more persistent than our acknowledgement of what we possess. Our clamoring is constant while our appreciation comes at widely separated moments.

How then can we cultivate the fine but difficult art of giving thanks regularly?

In one of his letters, Robert Southey tells of a Spaniard who always put on his spectacles when he was about to eat strawberries so that they might look bigger and more tempting. "In just the same way," adds Southey, "I make the most of my enjoyments."

At Sukkot time, we would do well to ponder these words. If only we could learn to magnify our blessings instead of exaggerating our troubles!

Grandma's eyesight wasn't as good as it used to be, but there was nothing wrong with her perspective. When asked about her health, she answered softly: "I have two teeth left, and thank God they are directly opposite one another." Her spectacles were properly focused.

Viewing our blessings in proper perspective means something else too—something which goes to the very heart of the art of giving thanks. A true perspective on our possessions serves to remind us that they are given to us in trust, to use not only for our own pleasures and gratification but also in the service of others. Gratitude at its highest goes beyond counting blessings. It involves sharing blessings. It leads not only to a sense of thankful dependence upon God but also to an awareness of our duty to our fellow-man. It talks not only of indebtedness to be acknowledged but also of debts to be discharged. It takes us beyond saying thanks to giving thanks.

On our festivals the Torah commands us to be joyous. The Hebrew word spelling out this injunction is *"Vesamahta"*—You Shall Rejoice. By a slight revocalization of the word, our Sages make it read *"Vesee-mahta"*—You Shall Cause to Rejoice. They then go on to remind us that we must use our festive days as occasions to bring joy into the lives of "the stranger, the orphan and the widow." We are not truly grateful until we make it possible for others to experience gratitude too.

This, after all, is what we really mean when we say "much obliged." We mean that we are much obligated, we have incurred a debt which we are duty bound to repay. What is involved is not generosity but common honesty.

The truth is that every blessing we enjoy has been sacrificially paid for by others. We are indebted far beyond our embarrassed means to make adequate recompense. It is no accident that the word "bless" and the word "bleed" come from the same root. Every important blessing we enjoy—our freedom, our health, our heritage, our security—is dipped in the blood of generations of benefactors. There is nothing we can give which we did not at first receive. Such obligations can never be fully liquidated. But neither are we exempt from making some sustained effort at repayment.

If we are truly thankful for our freedom we must be vitally concerned with the plight of those who still wear chains. If we are grateful for our share of God's abundance, we must share that abundance with the ill-fed, the ill-clad, the ill-housed. If we are genuinely appreciative of our own good health, the plight of the handicapped becomes a legitimate claim upon our financial resources. If we are sincere when we exclaim of our spiritual legacy, "happy are we, how goodly is our inheritance," then it becomes incumbent upon us to strengthen the institutions dedicated to disseminating a knowledge of Judaism.

The art of giving thanks means ultimately no appreciation without reciprocation.

The Three-Walled Sukkah

~∙~

A RABBINIC COMMENT on the Book of Job seems to be speaking to us most intimately at the *Yizkor* hour on Shemini Atzeret.

Job was a good man who suffered compound calamities. A Midrash tells us that "When Job complained about his misfortunes, the Holy One, blessed be He, showed him a Sukkah of three walls."

What was the Almighty trying to teach Job through this strange symbol? What would a three-walled Sukkah say to a man in the depths of despair and anguish?

We can only guess at what the author of this Midrash had in mind. Each of us can read different meanings into the enigmatic metaphor.

Let us suggest a few things it might say.

One message may be that the three-walled Sukkah is God's way of reminding Job that every person's Sukkah has one wall missing. Sure, everyone would like to have a four-walled Sukkah—a happy marriage, gifted children, a successful career, good health, and a long life. In actual life, however, no one has a four-walled Sukkah. Sorrow, failure, loss of health, disappointment—in varying degrees —these are our common human lot. There is a democracy in suffering—no one is exempt. You Job are not alone in your travails. Three-walled Sukkahs are the rule not the exception.

A second message is conveyed by the strange symbolism. Rabbinic law tells us that "a three-walled Sukkah is kosher for use" (on the holiday). Despite the missing wall, the Sukkah continues to stand. Somehow life goes on. Life, it has been observed, is full of heartbreak but it is also full of overcoming it.

In the first flush of sorrow we say, "Oh, I can never get over this, I cannot survive such a blow." But somehow we do survive and we do go on. In life, a piece of a wall falls away now, another piece at another time, but the Sukkah remains standing.

Which rabbi or counselor has not heard people cry out when the wound is raw, "how do I go on?" The only honest answer is, "I don't know how to go on but I do know that others have gone on and you are probably as wise, as brave, and as strong as they."

But if life is to go on, if we are to survive the collapse of a wall of our Sukkah we must learn to look at the three walls that are standing rather than at the one which has fallen. Some of us having sustained a grievous loss either of a loved one or a fortune cannot erase the loss from our minds. We keep talking about it, bemoaning it, weeping over it.

Harold Russell, the handless veteran of World War II, told us his story in a book ironically titled *Victory In My Hands*. One sentence in that book deserves to be held before every Job: "It's not what you have lost, but what you have left that counts."

So, God was saying to Job, stop thinking only of the pains you suffer, you also have pleasures to enjoy. Stop counting and recounting your losses, and begin counting your blessings. Sure you have lost a wall of your Sukkah but there are three walls remaining. Make the most of those three walls. You will be held accountable for what you do with those remaining walls.

And remember Job that you belong to a people which has mastered the art of surviving in a three-walled Sukkah. Your people survived the loss of a land, dispersion, persecution and bigotries of varying intensity and severity. Despite these multiple deprivations, your people retained their humanity, their compassion, their dedication to justice, and have extravagantly enriched an undeserving mankind in a measure grotesquely disproportionate to their meager numbers. We have shown the world how to live in a three-walled Sukkah.

And one last thing Job. Because a wall of your own Sukkah has collapsed, you have an unobstructed view of your neighbor's Sukkah. Look carefully and you will see he, too, is missing a wall in his Sukkah.

Perhaps this is why we come together to say Yizkor. As we look upon others remembering and memorializing, we are so vividly reminded that we all are knit together in the common brotherhood of pain and vulnerability. Another's pain does not lessen our own, but it may help to move us from self-pity to the healing which comes from trying to bind up the wounds of another.

In the blessing for the food which we recite after the meal on this festival we insert these words: "May the All-Merciful raise up for us the collapsed Sukkah of David." We look forward to the day when all Sukkot will be full and intact. Until that blessed day arrives we must make do each of us with a three-walled Sukkah and make that Sukkah as beautiful as we can.

The Secret of Our Immortality

WHEN YOU COME into a traditional synagogue on Simhat Torah evening, the sights and the sounds that will greet you will make you wonder whether you are, in fact, in a house of worship. The mood will range from gay to wild. The atmosphere will be charged with celebration. The occasion? Simhat Torah—Rejoicing in the Torah.

Here is what Herman Wouk, the renowned novelist, has written about this uniquely Jewish festival: "Nobody who has been in a synagogue during Simhat Torah needs to be told what it is like. For one who has never seen it, description will be pale. The manner varies from the exalted frenzy of the Hasidic congregations to the decorous dancing and singing in the elegant Manhattan synagogues. The essence everywhere is the same: excitement, singing, joking, joy within the usually solemn precincts of worship.

"Seven times, chanting processions circle the synagogue with all the Holy Torah Scrolls. Flag-waving children march behind in cheery disorder. . . . A powerful jubilation irradiates the synagogue. The time comes when the rabbi is himself drawn into the rejoicing and solemnly dances with a Holy Scroll in his arms. My grandfather, patriarchal and reserved all year long, was still performing this dance in his 90s, a few shuffling, tottering steps, his face alight with pleasure as he clasped the Torah in his old arms" (*This Is My God*, pages 79-80).

What is it that the flag-waving children and the tottering patriarch celebrate on Simhat Torah? They are celebrating first the privilege of having reached the annual conclusion of the Torah reading cycle. On Simhat Torah we read publicly the last verses of the Book of Deuteronomy. Then we begin immediately to read the Torah once again from Chapter 1, verse 1 of the Book of Genesis. Thus, we demonstrate our unending obligation to study Torah and to draw continuous inspiration from the living words of our sacred Scriptures.

Judaism is vitally concerned that we serve God with heart, soul and might. But it has been no less insistent that we serve Him too with our minds—with minds that stay open and keep growing.

As we grow older it is very tempting to develop a permanent mind set. But minds, like parachutes, are valuable only when open.

To shut the windows of the mind is to court mental and spiritual suffocation. We must literally never stop going to school, broadening our horizons and expanding our knowledge.

This is the distinctive Jewish contribution to mental hygiene—the unparalleled emphasis upon study as a process that only death ought to terminate.

As long as we keep our minds open and alert, as long as we are willing to try a new skill, entertain a new thought, develop a new friend, surrender an old prejudice—so long do we remain vital people, so long do we gain ground and move forward in the search for more abundant life.

On Simhat Torah we celebrate, too, the privilege that has been ours to be God's messengers on an exalted and perilous errand—to be the carriers of His word to humanity. The Torah earned for us the title "The People of the Book." The Torah is our mark of nobility, the central symbol of our historical adventure, the most potent source of our strength and the guarantor of our survival.

In 1898, Mark Twain wrote an article in *Harper's* magazine entitled "Concerning the Jews." There the following passage appears: "All things are mortal but the Jew; all other forces pass, but he remains. What is the secret of his immortality?"

The answer to Mark Twain's question is given every evening in our prayers: "The words of the Torah are our life and the length of our days." Should you enter a synagogue this evening you are very likely to hear these words chanted in Hebrew in joyous affirmation. And then your heart will guess the truth that you have discovered the secret of our immortality.

On Learning to Give Thanks

CICERO'S STATEMENT that gratitude is not only the greatest of virtues but the mother of them all, is one to which we instinctively nod in agreement. Giving thanks is, after all, no more than a question of good manners. One of the first phrases we teach the mumbling child is "thank you" so that the child might cultivate a sense of gratitude for pleasures and favors received. But on Thanksgiving Day we might pause to ask ourselves how often we feel a genuine sense of gratitude to Him whose lovingkindness is always with us.

Ziggy, whom some of us know from the cartoon world, was recently shown looking up toward the heavens as he says: "I don't mean to complain, but I think I've been reapin' a lot more than I ever had a chance to sow."

Ziggy's attitude is all too familiar. He is like most of us—complaining about the management of the universe, protesting that we're getting the short end of the stick.

A well-known legend tells of two angels, each given a basket and sent to earth to gather up the prayers that were offered there. One was to collect only man's petitions. The other was to gather up his prayers of gratitude. When they returned, the angel bearing the requests was carrying a basket filled to overflowing. The other angel was deeply depressed for his basket was all but empty.

The angels might very well have performed their mission among us in this land of vastly disproportionate good fortune.

One of the built-in hazards of being human is the overpowering temptation to greet success in a mood of self-congratulation. The weeds of pride flourish most conspicuously in the soil of prosperity. The Bible speaks of the pride which goes before a fall. It would be no less in order to call attention to the pride which comes after a rise. When life becomes comfortable and upholstered, when our undertakings prosper and our possessions multiply, we are so prone to proclaim ourselves self-made. What further demonstration do we need of our resourcefulness, our wisdom, our ingenuity, our cleverness?

How well Moses understood the need to caution against the all too prevalent tendency to regard our blessings as proof of our ability or our virtue: "Beware, lest you forget the Lord your God. . . . Lest when you have eaten and are satisfied you say in your heart: 'My power and the might of my hand has gotten me this wealth.' " Apparently, Little Jack Horner was not the only one to become persuaded that he was really a very good boy simply because he had managed to pull a few plums out of life's pie. It never occurred to him to reserve a kind thought or word for the one who had baked the pie or the One who made the plums to grow.

It is supremely significant that the ancient Biblical festival of thanksgiving, the festival of Sukkot, which served as a model for the pilgrims, was born not in mighty prosperous Rome, nor in secure, amply endowed Greece. Thanksgiving had its origin in weak, insecure and tiny Judea. The poet was undoubtedly correct in speaking of "the glory that was Greece and the grandeur that was Rome." But while Greece enjoyed glory and Rome was resplendent in grandeur, it was lowly Judea that had gratitude.

Nor should we forget the bleak background against which the pilgrims marked their first Thanksgiving. Of the 102 passengers who landed at Plymouth Rock, 51 died within the first six months. Their graves had to be kept level with the ground in order to save them from desecration and to keep from the Indians the knowledge of the frightful toll of casualties. Not a single family had been spared by death. The survivors lived on the fringe of starvation in a hostile, unchartered world. They never knew what it was to have enough or to be secure. They stood alone against the forces of nature and man. These were the people who gathered to give thanks to Almighty God for His blessings and to express their humble dependence upon His mercies for their continuing life.

We need to approach our greater blessings in a similar mood.

Have we indeed created ourselves? Is it our genius which fashioned that most intricate of all miracles—the complex and wonderful mechanism we know as the human body?

Have we set the stars in their courses or commanded the sun to rise and set? Has our wisdom made the seed or taught it how to yield the golden grain and the luscious fruit? Have we taught the birds to sing or the waves to dance?

Did we create the air which surrounds us or the breathing apparatus which sustains us? Has our blood purchased the freedom we enjoy?

Can we make even so fragmentary a list of our blessings without becoming submerged by an overpowering and profound sense of gratitude?

A good Thanksgiving Day exercise might consist of sitting down with two sheets of paper. On one we ought to list all the things we crave and are yearning to acquire. On the other sheet we ought to enumerate all those things we own and could lose. To our surprise we would find the first list quickly exhausted while the second would appear endless. We would probably soon tear up the first list, feeling a little ashamed and largely thankful.

Every day is Thanksgiving Day on the calender of the religious Jew. We are obliged to recite no fewer than 100 blessings each day. Perhaps we might add one prayer of petition:

"Thou hast given so much to me,
Give me one thing more—a grateful heart."

On Being Impractical

WHEN A CONGREGANT was informed by her rabbi that the first Hanukkah candle will be lit that year on the evening of December 10th, she exclaimed, "Hanukkah is surely early this year!" "No, it isn't," the rabbi hastened to assure her. "Hanukkah is precisely on time. It begins this year, as it always does, on the 25th day of the Hebrew month Kislev."

Whenever Hanukkah comes it brings a soft glow and warmth which help take the edge off December's frosty bite. And the flickering candles have a special bit of wisdom they would share with us.

After we recite the blessings which accompany the lighting of the candles, we add a prayer in which there is this striking sentence: "These candles are sacred and we are not permitted to put them to any use; we may only look upon them."

Let's understand what the prayer declares. We may not use the Hanukkah candles for any practical purpose. We may not read by their light. We may not use them to light the Shabbat candles. In fact we may not use one Hanukkah candle to light another one. That is why we use the *Shamash* candle.

How terribly impractical all this sounds especially to us who live in a utilitarian society, who measure the value of all things by one pragmatic question: "What is it good for?" The light of the Hanukkah candles, tradition tells us, is not to be used for anything; it is just for looking.

It figures. After all, how practical were the people to whom we owe the festival of Hanukkah? They were the most impractical people. There were others, much more practical, who said: "Why resist the Syrians, the bearers of the proud Greek culture? They are the wave of the future. Why should we be different? Why can't we be just like everybody else?"

These practical people were called Hellenists. They spoke the Greek language, dressed like Greeks, participated in Greek sports, adopted Greek names, neglected Hebrew, Shabbat, *Yom Tov*, and gradually replaced them by pagan observances. Had these practical people prevailed they would have sounded the death-knell of Judaism.

Happily there were some very impractical Jews in the year 168 B.C.E. Mattathias spoke for them when he declared: "Though all the heathen within the bounds of the royal domain obey him [Antiochus] and each one forsakes the worship of his fathers . . . yet will I, my sons and my brothers walk in the covenant of our fathers."

This may be the real miracle of Hanukkah—that there were enough impractical people who believed that security purchased at the cost of conscience is too dearly purchased; impractical people, ill-trained and ill-equipped who dared to take on a foe far more mighty and more numerous; impractical people who followed the line of most resistance and, like the saying goes, "would rather fight than switch."

And if we are here more than 2100 years later still celebrating Hanukkah it is because in all the intervening years there were enough impractical Jewish mothers and fathers, humble, nameless heroes and heroines, who often at great peril and in the most forbidding circumstances, kindled the Hanukkah lights, looked at them and knew who they were and what was expected of them.

A streak of impracticality runs through Jewish thought as well as Jewish history. Thus one of the truly unique Jewish contributions is the concept of *"Torah lishmah"*—study of Torah for its own sake. We are urged to engage in a discipline of study which leads to no trade or profession, which has no utilitarian purpose, which we may not use "as a spade with which to dig"—to use the rabbinic phrase. Torah study directed to no practical end is one of our tradition's most hallowed *Mitzvot*.

We are also urged to serve God without any practical purpose in mind. Our performance of His will should be motivated solely by our love of Him and not by any hope that we will be repaid by material blessings. Thus we are admonished in *Pirkei Avot* (Ethics of Our Fathers): "Be not like servants who serve their Master for the sake of receiving a reward. Be rather like those servants who serve their Master without expecting a reward." A *Mitzvah* is not an investment on which dividends are expected. "The reward of the *Mitzvah* is the *Mitzvah* itself." Beyond that, it has no practical value.

When we stop to think about the matter we realize how deeply indebted we are to impractical people. Giving charity is impractical. After all, why should anyone voluntarily part with possessions acquired at the cost of time and toil? Giving time to one's synagogue or community is impractical. The time could be used for one's own entertainment, recreation or relaxation. Visiting the sick, comforting the bereaved, performing acts of kindness and thoughtfulness are all impractical—the time and energy could be better invested in furthering our own pursuits. Yet who will deny that it is precisely these impractical acts which humanize our lives and add a dimension of holiness to our existence?

So as we kindle the Hanukkah lights this year let's just look at them. Remember, they have no practical value. Or do they?

"You Shall Plant"

IN HIS EARLY efforts to persuade the Sultan of Turkey to grant the Zionists a charter authorizing them to colonize Palestine, Theodor Herzl enlisted the sympathetic aid of Kaiser Wilhelm of Germany. In 1898 the Kaiser visited Palestine and he accorded Dr. Herzl an informal reception outdoors.

In the course of the conversation Herzl asked: "Has the land of our dreams found grace in your eyes, Your Majesty?"

The Kaiser replied: "It is impossible to dream here, the heat is unbearable. The land must be shaded, it must be covered with woods."

"We are not permitted," sighed Herzl, "the land is not in our hands."

Whereupon the Kaiser remarked: "The land will belong to the people that will shade it and cover its barrenness with trees."

Planting trees has been an age-old passion with the Jews. It derived its major impetus from the Biblical verse: "When you come into the land, you shall plant all manner of trees . . ." (Lev. 23:19).

Unique among all the religions of the world Judaism included in its calendar a holiday dedicated to the planting of trees. Tu bi-Shevat, the 15th day of the Hebrew month Shevat, is considered the "New Year for the Trees." It has always been observed as a day for eating fruits grown in the Holy Land. In modern times, when Jews began to restore the homeland, Tu bi-Shevat gained the added significance of Arbor Day, a time for planting trees.

Unusual as the holiday itself, is the fact that it should have been preserved at all by diaspora Jews who had virtually no relationship with the land. What is more, Tu bi-Shevat which marks the beginning of spring in the Holy Land, comes in the dead of winter in most lands where Jews live.

All the more remarkable, therefore, is the incredible passion with which the Jews applied themselves to the sacred task of covering the barrenness of the homeland.

When Mark Twain visited Palestine in 1867 he described it as "desolate and unlovely. It is a hopeless, dreary, heartbroken land." Several decades later Clarence Darrow wrote: "Palestine is a land of sand and stones, and the stones are there to keep the sand from blowing away." If only they and the Kaiser could see today what a marvelous rebirth that land has enjoyed as loving hands nursed it back to health and life.

In all the annals of mankind there is no record of a land having changed so radically, so swiftly, as deserts and swamps were transformed into fields and forests, parks and pastures. The people of Israel have planted more than 150 million trees where not very long ago Darrow found only sand and stones.

Who could have foretold that the land, long dead, choked beneath the hot desert sands that had been permitted to suffocate it, was destined for a marvelous resurrection? It seems indeed that, as Israel Zangwill wrote: "The land without a people was waiting for the people without a land." Stubbornly, patiently, courageously, lovingly, the Jew has reclaimed his beloved soil. He washed away her salt and sand. He drained her marshes and swamps. He wiped out her malaria and trachoma. He healed the scars of century-old neglect.

David Ben Gurion, Israel's first Prime Minister, understood the urgency of the task of reclamation and summoned his people with a mixture of eloquence, wisdom and passion in a message which still thrills us: "...We are an entirely new state which has to make up for the neglect of generations, for sins against our people as well as our country.... The mountains of our country still stand naked and pray for the hand of the planter to restore their pristine woods and forests.... We are under no obligation to accept the heritage of desolation from the past, for it is within our power to fertilize the sand dunes, to dig wells, to exploit the hidden resources, to build and to revive the dust of the earth, to redeem its minerals and natural resources." Indeed, this is the true conquest of the land; this, indeed, is the great mission which the Jewish National Fund is called upon to undertake in our own day.

In this effort to effect "the true conquest of the land" Jews throughout the world joined enthusiastically. Even before the emergence of the state, when Jewish settlements began to take root in the land, diaspora Jews began sending money for trees. Many of us grew up in homes where the Jewish National Fund "blue box" stood alongside of other "*pushkes*," which were the weekly recipients of coins before the Friday night candles were lit.

Many of us have childhood memories of rattling those same blue boxes in subway cars and on street corners as we eagerly solicited coins to help plant trees in the ancient land.

Planting trees from afar has become a widespread practice among Jews everywhere. Trees in memory of loved ones, trees in honor of the birth of a child or granchild, trees in honor of a birthday or a graduation. Tu bi-Shevat has become a holiday to be observed all year round.

One of the thrilling experiences in our time is to plant a sapling with one's own hands in the soil of Israel. The Jewish National Fund equips the planter with a folder which contains a prayer to be offered either in Hebrew or in translation:

> "Take pleasure, O Lord, in Your land
> And bestow upon it of Your goodness and Your grace.
> Give dew for a blessing
> And cause beneficent rains to fall in their season,
> To satiate the mountains of Israel and her valleys,
> And to water thereon every plant and tree
> And these saplings
> Which we plant before You this day."

Purim's Sobering Lessons

"PURIM IZ NIT kein yom tov und kadoches iz nit kein krenk." "Purim is not a festival and fever is no disease." This Yiddish folk adage contains a mighty dose of disrespect, or at least irreverence, for the festival of Purim.

The Book of Esther which contains the story of Purim is the only Biblical book which does not contain as much as a single mention of God's name. And the book had to go through quite a struggle before it became part of the Bible.

The hero and heroine in the story, Mordecai and Esther, have names that sound suspiciously like Marduk and Istar, Babylonian deities.

And most damaging to Purim's claim to honor is the disconcerting fact that few modern scholars are prepared to accept the Purim story as authentic history. The narrative appears too contrived to be accorded credibility. It is more likely the product of a creative imagination than the chronicle of an historian.

Despite the aspersions that were cast on Purim, this spiritual vagabond of questionable legitimacy, the Jews welcomed Purim with a warmth and gaiety they did not lavish upon the more austere holidays with untainted pedigrees.

Perhaps the Jew could more readily identify with Purim because he too was considered a vagabond among the nations, he too was vilified, he too had his legitimacy challenged. Whatever the reason, the Jew welcomed Purim into his home and heart, and made its arrival the occasion for a degree of merrymaking he never permitted himself in the presence of the more respectable visitors.

Moreover, the tradition which is so heavily committed to sobriety made it almost obligatory to consume so much alcohol on Purim that one could no longer distinguish "blessed be Mordecai" from "cursed be Haman."

(Characteristically, before the Jew was allowed to overindulge, he was obliged to remember the poor with gifts. Somewhat reminiscent is the sign at a mid-city bar: "If you are drinking to forget, please pay in advance.")

Even the synagogue whose sanctity was so inviolate all year round, became on Purim the scene of noisy celebrations that were decidedly off limits on other festivals.

Thus Purim, in spite of its humble rank among the festivals, this buck-private among the brass, received a thunderous reception from a people who were usually harried and harassed and welcomed an opportunity to make merry.

And perhaps Purim was welcomed because it served other purposes as well. Amidst the mandated inebriety, the Jew absorbed from Purim some very sobering lessons.

He stood taller when he read of the courage of Mordecai who would not bow down nor kneel before Haman. Here was this prime minister, next to the king the most powerful representative of a most powerful empire, before whom all bowed in submissive obeisance. One person alone, Mordecai, denies him adoration. The Sages embellished the narrative by explaining the reason for Mordecai's refusal to bow before Haman. Haman, they say, wore an idol on his chest, thus Mordecai's very faith in God was at stake. He risked the wrath of a vengeful prime minister rather than appear to compromise his most cherished belief.

Has this not been the role of the Jew through the centuries? Has he not been the perpetual dissenter against every political and religious totalitarianism that secular and religious rules have sought to impose upon men? When Hellenism or Rome or the church or the mosque demanded complete conformity and tried to impose a coercive uniformity, was it not the Jew who alone resisted these imperialisms, the Jew who served as the lone heckler in a mass chorus, the Jew who was repeatedly the Mordecai who would not bow down?

There was another lesson the Jew absorbed from Purim. The Purim story taught him how inextricably the destiny of the individual Jew is intertwined with the fate of all Jews. Here Haman was offended by a single person, Mordecai. But when he learns that Mordecai is a Jew "it seemed contemptible in his eyes to lay hands on Mordecai alone. . . . Wherefore Haman sought to destroy all the Jews that were throughout the whole kingdom of Ahasuerus." A single Jews pricks his pride and Haman is ready to destroy them all.

Mordecai himself stresses the same theme of Jewish interdependence a little later in the story. When he urges Esther to intercede with the king on behalf of her people she hesitates because she says that she risks losing her life by coming to the king uninvited. Whereupon Mordecai warns her: "Think not to thyself that thou shalt escape in the king's house more than all the Jews." Esther's special status will not exempt her from the fate of her people. Tyranny draws no distinctions between Jews. Even when we do not share a common faith we share a common fate. Elementary wisdom, therefore, dictates that our single destiny should strengthen the bonds of concern, compassion and caring for each other.

The last thing that Purim taught the Jew was an unwavering faith in Jewish survival. It was this faith that Mordecai expressed when he told Esther that if she does not act to save her people "help and rescue will come to the Jews from somewhere else." Mordecai did not say, nor perhaps did he know, where that "somewhere else" was. One thing he knew for sure. His people would live on. They are an eternal people whom no tyrant can defeat and no empire can vanquish. "I shall not die but live and declare the works of the Lord," says the Psalmist.

And so it has been. Many a tyrant who attempted to destroy the Jewish people is remembered only because he linked his name malevolently with the story of an undying people.

Purim's message unfortunately was always timely. Always there lurked some threat to Jewish survival, and the Jew was reassured and strengthened by the bright hope and sparkling faith of Purim.

So treasured are the lessons of Purim that the great Maimonides taught that when the Messiah comes all the festivals will be abolished—except Purim.

Historians might question whether the events of the Purim story are authentic. For us, Jews, Purim's lessons remain abidingly true.

I Love Pesaḥ Best of All

COMING EVENTS cast their shadows before them and what a long shadow Pesah casts. So it is not too soon to confess that, if I may parody a once popular song, I love Pesah in the springtime, I love Pesah best of all.

Yes, I am powerfully partial to Pesah. It's my favorite on the Jewish calendar.

Mind you, I have nothing against the other holidays and holy days. They each have their own appeal to my heart. But Pesah . . . ah, Pesah is special.

Nor do I think that I am alone in this partisanship. I suspect the Bible of playing favorites with Pesah. How else explain the fact that it did not command us to retell the story behind any other festival?

No less than four times does the Bible enjoin: tell your children about Pesah. About the others, not a whisper. We are under no obligation to explain why we observe Rosh Hashanah or Shavuot, but Pesah alone has a *Haggadah*.

I also suspect the Jewish people as a whole of belonging to the Pesah Fan Club. Did you ever hear a Jew called Hanukkah or Yom Kippur or Hamishah Asar bi-Shevat? But we have heard of many Jews called Pesah, haven't we? Moreover, even the month during which Pesah occurs—Nisan—became a Jewish name. No other month on the Jewish calendar can make that claim.

And so, as I said, I think that I am in crowded company when I confess that my heart belongs to Pesah. Let me try to explain the reasons for the romance.

In the first place, I love the *mood* of Pesah. It comes at the season when the earth discards its bleak winter garments and dresses itself in its most alluring colors. On Pesah we read the Biblical love book, The Song of Songs, which captures the lyric, joyous rhythm of the aliveness, the wonder, the miracle of springtime:

"For lo, the winter is past . . .
The flowers appear on the earth
The time of singing has come . . .
The fig tree puts forth her green figs,
And the vines in blossom give forth their fragrance."

With the rebirth of nature, hope is reborn, faith is rekindled, the step is a little livelier, the greeting more cheerful. In April, God seems to be doing an encore for us who were not present at the dawn of creation.

April is the easiest time of the year to believe in God. I think there are no atheists in April. The blooming flowers, the symphonic birds, the frolicking sunbeams, all unite to persuade us: "God's in His heaven, all's right with the world."

In the second place, I love the *meaning* of Pesah. It tells of a God who wants man to be free. He is a God who hears the groaning of the slaves and sends a messenger to remind them in their agony that their cries have been heard.

He is a God who threatens destruction upon every tyrant who hardens his heart to the call of compassion and the demands of justice. He is a God who reveals Himself to the humiliated, the despised, the oppressed.

When He proclaims His commandments, He introduces Himself by saying: "I am the Lord your God who brought you out of the land of Egypt, out of the house of bondage." This is His signature. He is a God of freedom.

God spoke to our people first about freedom. Ever since, freedom has spoken with a Jewish accent. Pesah renews our faith in the coming of a day when all will be free, and Pesah rekindles our determination to work for that day.

In the third place, I love the *method* of Pesah. It activates us. It makes demands upon us. It puts us to work. Change the dishes!

...my mother was when I disobeyed; not until I became a
...d I know how proud my mother was when I achieved; not
...ecame a mother did I realize how much my mother loves

...time to time we score an imaginary triumph over another
...being, and we gloat in self-congratulation: "Boy, did I put
...his place." Pesah reminds us that there is something far more
...e than putting another person in his place and that is putting
...rself in his place. This happens to be excellent counsel, not only
...esah time, but all through the year.

Order the *Matzot* and the wine! Clean the house! Get rid of the *hametz*! Invite the family! Make sure David knows the four questions. Get Ruthie new shoes and a new hat for mother. Let's see, now, how many *Haggadot* will we need?

Pesah is not a holiday you confront casually. You have to prepare carefully and diligently.

When the *Seder* finally arrives, we keep busy. We are all involved. Mother, father, grandparents, children are all actors in a great drama of liberation. Each has lines to speak, songs to sing and a role to play.

And the symbolic foods of the *Seder* help us to relive and recapture our past. Israel Zangwill correctly said, "On Pesah the Jew eats history." This food, this "bread of affliction" becomes the bread of our salvation. It nourishes our loyalties to our tradition, our love for our people, and our joy in living as Jews.

Finally, I love the *message* of Pesah. It is striking, when you stop to think of it, that the festival of freedom imposes the most restraints and the most restrictions.

On Pesah we are least free in our choice of what we may eat and where we may eat. Pesah calls for self-discipline. It demands obedience to law and tradition. Without these, the message of freedom evaporates.

The sad truth about many of us is that though we live in the freest country in the world we are held in bondage by inner pharaohs who rule over us. Some of us are enslaved by the pharaoh of tyrannical habits. Some of us are the serfs of the pharaoh of prejudice and greed. Some of us pay excessive tribute to the pharaoh of success or pleasure.

The invisible chains these despots fashion are as real as any imposed by a human dictator. Pesah calls upon us to discipline ourselves, to take control over our lives, and to remove the shackles we ourselves have forged.

And so for all these things—for its mood, its meaning, its method and its message—I love Pesah in the springtime! I love Pesah best of all!

Let's Pretend

PESAH IS SUPPOSED to be "the season of our freedom," but as a matter of fact, no holiday finds us less free to do what we want than Pesah. Our diet is rigidly prescribed by tradition, the *Haggadah* provides the words we are to speak, the songs we are to sing, the memories we are to recall. And Pesah comes perilously close to exercising thought control.

Thus, the *Haggadah* commands: "In every generation man is obliged to look upon himself as though he personally went out of Egypt." Notice the impact of that injunction. We are obliged to do more than eat the foods the Hebrew slaves ate and retell the drama of their liberation. We are supposed to think of ourselves as though we ourselves were the slaves. It is we who felt the taskmaster's lash; ours were the tears mixed with the mortar; ours were the cries and the groans a merciful God heard; ours were the bent backs that became straight in the flight from slavery. We have to think ourselves into Egypt. We must look upon ourselves as though.... Let's pretend....

Tradition summons us in this magnificent exhortation to develop one of the most crucial qualities for humane, compassionate living—a sympathetic imagination that enables us to put ourselves in the place of another human being. This was what Walt Whitman had in mind when he said: "I never ask the wounded person how he feels; I myself become the wounded person." Let's pretend.

And this is what our Sages m
"Do not judge your fellow

The poet Shelley once sa
good, must imagine intense
himself in the place of anoth
pleasures of his species must be

There is a desperate shortage in
this quality which Judaism prescrib
thetic imagination to enable us to get
skin.

There would be more harmony in the
to understand the fears, the dilemmas, th
and if parents would try to imagine the a
growing up.

Sermons would sound less self-righteous if ra
themselves into a pew. And congregants would be
could sympathetically put themselves in the rabbi's

Hospital patients would get more thoughtful treat
physicians were obliged to spend one week a year in a h
And perhaps patients would be more understanding of the
if they could follow them on their harassing and demandi
rounds.

More of us would visit parents and grandparents in old-age ho
if we could project ourselves into those bleak institutions and try
understand how much a visit can relieve the burden of loneliness and
a sense of being unwanted.

"If we could read the secret history of our enemies," wrote Long-
fellow, "we should find in each man's life sorrow and suffering
enough to disarm all hostility."

It would be easier to raise money for Israel Bonds if we were more
amply endowed with the ability to see ourselves as inhabitants of the
besieged and beleaguered State of Israel.

More of us would wield our pens and raise our voices on behalf of
Soviet Jewry if we could imagine ourselves as Russian Jews waiting
desperately for liberation from the prison which is Soviet Russia. "In
every generation a man is obliged to look upon himself as though...."

Victoria Farnsworth touched a very sensitive nerve when she
wrote: "Not until I became a mother did I understand how much my
mother had sacrificed for me; not until I became a mother did I feel

how hurt
mother d
until I b
me."

Fro
huma
him
nob
you
at

The King of Kings and I

ON SAINT THOMAS ISLAND there is a mountain that dominates the beautiful landscape. One place which affords a breathtaking view of the land and the sea is called appropriately "Lookout Point." A sign erected there by a real estate company carries this legend:

> "View—Courtesy of Scott-Free Estates.
> With a little help from God."

That sign echoes a rabbinic comment on the song of thanksgiving which our ancestors sang after they crossed in safety the sea which separated them from the Egyptian bondage which lay behind them and the beckoning freedom that lay ahead of them.

In their relief and exuberance they proclaimed: "This is my God and I will glorify Him. . . ."

Our ancient Sages probed this passage and asked how does one glorify God? Can a mere mortal add even one shred of glory to Him whose glory already fills the whole world?

A variety of answers were offered to this question. One Sage took the single Hebrew word which means "and I will glorify Him"—*V'anveyhu*—and broke it into two Hebrew words—*anee v'hu*—meaning "I and He."

"I and He"—a great partnership. Man and God are joined together in a wide variety of sacred enterprises, and they are desperately dependent upon each other.

A young lad reminded a rather pompous farmer of one-half of this truth. The farmer was showing the boy his acreage and bragged extravagantly about his accomplishments. He concluded his monologue of self-congratulation with the proud boast: "I grew it all by myself, Sonny. And I started out with nothing!"

"With nothing?" the young fellow asked in amazement. "Golly, sir, without even a seed?"

An agricultural college in Iowa did a study on the production of 100 bushels of corn on one acre of land. The farmer contributed the labor. God contributed a few things too:

> 4,000,000 pounds of water
> 6,800 pounds of oxygen
> 5,200 pounds of carbon
> 125 pounds of potassium
> 160 pounds of nitrogen
> 1900 pounds of carbon dioxide
> 75 pounds of yellow sulphur
> 50 pounds of calcium
> 40 pounds of phosphorous
> 2 pounds of iron and smaller amounts of iodine, zinc, copper and other things.

And, oh yes, there was the small matter of sunshine.

All for 100 bushels of corn.

Who made them? "I and He."

"God," wrote Abraham Lincoln, "is the silent partner in all great enterprises." This, we should add, includes moral enterprises no less than those involving nature.

The other side of this coin involves a more daring truth. Just as man depends upon God, so does God depend upon man. "I and He." God can no more do without us than we can do without Him.

Even the Pesaḥ story was interpreted by our Sages in such a way that the miracle of the parting of the sea was not a solo performance by the Almighty. The Israelites made their vital contribution. Thus our Sages said: "The sea did not part for them until they entered the waters up to their nostrils." Without the courage and the faith of the Israelites who ventured into the menacing sea, there would have been no miracle. "I and He."

Perhaps it may sound blasphemous or irreverent but a mature understanding of God must include an awareness of how much God needs us. As children we were taught to believe that God is omnipotent, that He can do everything. Well, there are a whole host of things that God cannot do—without us.

There is not a single affliction from which we suffer—war, poverty, pollution, injustice, racial strife—that God can remove without our cooperation.

There is not a single blessing we crave—world peace, food and shelter for all, clean air, a just society—that God can bring without our cooperation.

Our view of God looks upon Him neither as a miracle worker, nor a magician who can provide instant cures for all the world ills. God is the Power who works in us and through us to enable us to achieve those things that our faith in Him assures us are capable of coming into being. "I and He."

God helps the poor with the charity we give; He heals the sick with the skill and support we provide; He cheers the lonely with the visits we make; He comforts the bereaved with the words we speak; He guides our children with the examples we set; He ennobles our lives with the good deeds we perform.

"We and God," wrote William James, "have business with each other and in that business our highest destiny is fulfilled."

Rabbi Ben Zion Bokser has written a poem in which he addressed himself to this God-man partnership:

GOD WROTE HALF

I composed a song about life,
But God wrote half.
He gave me wings,
I soared on high
And saw the world.
I acclaimed love
And derided hate,
But He guided my heart
To choose.
He gave me a joy and a pain,
My spirit brooded on them,
And they released a light.
Time turned what I knew into words,
The words came together
And gave birth
To the song.

Remembering the Six Million

IN RECENT YEARS a melancholy observance has been added to the Jewish calendar—Yom Hashoah, Holocaust Day. On the 27th day of Nisan we pause to mark the unspeakable tragedy of the murder of the Six Million.

If the truth be told, not too many Jews are aware that such a day for remembering these Six Million victims has been added to the Jewish calendar in our own lifetime. Fewer still pause to mark it in any way.

We can understand why most of us would rather not be reminded of this most disastrous chapter in the history of a people which is no stranger to suffering. The subject is as painful as it is incomprehensible. To invoke the memories of those who perished in the gas chambers, in the ovens and in the mass graves, is to reopen wounds which have not yet healed; it is to raise unanswerable questions about man and God.

But remember the Six Million we must. That is the very least we owe them—the immortality which remembrance confers. We are their refuge against oblivion. If we do not remember them, they die a second time. As we remember them, we deny Hitler a posthumous victory.

On the wall of Yad Vashem, the overpowering Holocaust memorial in Jerusalem, there are inscribed these words from *Neder* ("The Vow") by Abraham Shlonsky:

"... I vow to remember as long as I live,
Forgiveness to me is lost as an art.
... I promise not to unlearn and later regret
But to inscribe and remember all that I saw."

Nor is it for the sake alone of the Six Million that we must re-member. The world needs to be reminded. After the close of the Eichmann trial, the *New York Times* asked editorially: "What was the object and justification of the trial?" The answer it gave to this question is worth pondering. "It was and it is to do all that can be done to eradicate an evil thing out of our civilization ... a thing so incredibly wicked that it would not have been believable of modern man if it had not actually occurred. This evil, this wickedness began with intolerance and hate in a few men's hearts. It spread until it almost wrecked the world. Now the obligation is to remember, not in hate, not in the spirit of revenge, but so that this spirit cannot ever flourish again so long as man remains on earth. And to this end, let us begin, each of us, by looking into our own hearts."

These are words that could bear reprinting periodically in news-papers throughout the world.

We must remember the Six Million for their sake, for the sake of the world and not least, for our own sake. Yes, for our own sake.

We Jews are a people who learned how to use our Egyptian bondage so that the agony of slavery was redeemed by the deepened moral sensitivity we derived from it. We can use even Dachau and Auschwitz if from it we, the living, derive a deeper loyalty to our people and to our faith.

There are two things, it seems, that we can do. In the first place we need more Jews. We need larger Jewish families. To all young people still planning their families we say: Every Jewish child that is born constitutes our most dramatic frustration of the enemies of our people.

In Gloria Goldreich's *The Four Days*, one of her women is debat-ing whether she should go through with a pregnancy. Her mother, a survivor, says to her: "Every Jewish baby that is born is a slap in Hitler's face."

Our answer to death is life. *"Lo amut kee ehyeh,"* "I shall not die but live." This is a great country with plenty of room for healthy children to grow in, and no group has given America more intelligent children, more sober and more law-abiding children than we have. As we raise larger families, America will be the richer, our lives will be the fuller, and our people's future more secure.

In addition to needing more Jews we need better Jews—that means us, you and I. With more than one-third of our people destroyed we must each take upon ourselves an added measure of responsibility. The prayers they might have offered, we must offer. The books they might have created and read, we must create and read. The Shabbat candles they would have kindled, we must kindle. The *tzedakah* they would have given, we must give. Every day, in every way, we must be more devout, more devoted, more dedicated.

Our honored dead could not save their own lives, but if we and all people remember them, they may be able to save and to deepen ours.

What Israel Means to Us

AS JEWS WHO ARE profoundly involved in Israel's destiny we tend to look at the State from the perspective of daily crises. We live by the headlines. And because good news is no news and usually goes unreported, Israel provides every loyal Jew with more than a fair share of heartaches. A characteristic Jewish telegram, one wit tells us, reads as follows: "Start worrying. Letter follows."

But when we mark once again an anniversary of Israel's rebirth we are not only entitled to the joy that all celebrations bring, we also owe it to ourselves to look at Israel in its larger perspective. What is the real meaning of Israel to world Jewry?

Coming so soon after the Holocaust the first thing that Israel did was to take the *"krechtz"* out of Jewish living! It has given Jews everywhere a mighty banner around which to rally—a banner not a tombstone. It has made Jews everywhere feel, as did our ancestors for other reasons, that being a Jew is a proud privilege.

A specific example is Karl Shapiro, a most gifted American poet. Until the rebirth of Israel, he was cited prominently as illustrating a tendency to total assimilation in American Jewry. In fact, his poetry echoed Christian motifs and reflected Jewish self-hatred. Again and again he struck out against his people. But came the birth of Israel and within a month Karl Shapiro wrote in the *New Yorker*: "When I think of the liberation of Zion, I hear the drop of chains. . . . I feel the weight of prisons in my skull falling away. . . .

When I see the name of Israel high in print the fences crumble in my flesh. . . . I say my name aloud for the first time unconsciously. . . . Speak the name of the land, speak the name only of the living land."

Yes, "the name of the living land," and this alone, could awaken the dormant yearning in estranged Jewish hearts. Jews everywhere have heard the drop of chains and have felt the weight of prisons fall away. They walk the earth with a newly discovered sense of pride and self-respect. In brief, Israel has not only taken many Jews out of exile; it has already taken the exile out of the Jew. That is the first meaning of Israel.

Israel has done something more for us—something so subtle that it could easily be overlooked. It has reversed the 2000-year-old role of the Jew on the stage of history. For the past two millennia the Jew's external history has been shaped for him by other nations. Coercion, subjugation, oppression, persecution, exile, martyrdom —these were the involuntary roles assigned to him. Jewish history has been for 2000 years not the story of what the Jew did as much as what was done to him. This motif of helplessness and passivity reached its frightening crescendo in the death of the Six Million.

Seen against this background, the rebirth of Israel points to a new role that the Jew has chosen for himself. He is saying to the world: "No more shall my destiny be shaped by the unkind hands of others. I have had enough—dear world too much—of playing the anvil for your hammer blows. Once upon a time my ancestors called themselves Maccabees because 'Maccab' means a hammer. Once again I shall beat out my own destiny, I shall forge for myself the instruments of my salvation. I shall honestly, stubbornly and unflinchingly rebuild myself in body and spirit on my ancestral soil which bloomed when my fathers tilled it, lay waste for centuries in alien hands and which has awakened once more to the tender caress of loving hands."

That is the meaning of Israel. That is the central meaning. A people is on the march, not a forced march, but a self-willed march. It has gotten off its knees and straightened its shoulders stooped by the burdens of the long night of exile and is standing erect. The spirit of the Maccabees has been rekindled. Israel has redeemed not only the land but more especially itself.

Finally, the rebirth of Israel has meant the rebirth of our faith in the power of ideals. It has reaffirmed our faith in the reality of spiritual forces in the world. It has rekindled our belief in miracles.

Who would have dared to believe possible what we have seen with our own eyes? Any "realistic" student of history could have advanced a thousand cogent reasons to deny the possibility of such a consummation. For here was a people divorced from its land for almost 2000 years, exposed to the corrosive acids of human brutality, a people whose very existence was called into question by a historian who labelled it a "fossil," a people whose dreams of restoration had been mocked by circumstance and even repudiated by many of its own members. That such a people could achieve the fulfillment of its most cherished and long-deferred hope at the precise moment when the hand of despair lay most heavily upon it—this is an achievement to convert the most skeptical and cynical of men into passionate believers in the invincibility of the human spirit when wedded to an imperishable ideal.

In the face of a miracle of such incredible dimensions, our will to believe receives most powerful stimulation. With the rebirth of Israel there has been reborn the faith of decent men and women everywhere that God is not mocked, that ultimately it is "not by might and not by power but by My spirit, says the Lord of Hosts."

Thus, on the anniversay of Israel's rebirth, we salute our brethren. We say to them: "Thank you for making us proud of you and thereby restoring to us our sense of pride. Thank you, too, for charting a new and more dignified role for our people—the role of a people determined to forge its own glorious destiny in justice and equity. And, above all, thank you for reviving our faith in all that is beautiful and worthwhile in life."

Making Today Count

"YOU SHALL COUNT from the day following the day of rest . . . seven full weeks shall be counted . . ." (Lev. 23:15-16).

The 49 days that separate Pesah from Shavuot are counted days. Beginning with the second night of Pesah and on each evening for the following seven weeks we recite a blessing as we count each day by number. When the seven weeks are completed we usher in the Festival of Shavuot, the Festival of Weeks.

The 33rd day of *Sephira*, of counting, is observed as a special day, a day of rejoicing, because on this day, according to tradition, a plague that had ravaged Rabbi Akiva's pupils was stayed.

This tradition of counting days for so long a time cannot help but convey to us the importance of each day of our lives, and the importance of making each day count. Almost inevitably we hear in this practice an echo of the prayer of the Psalmist: "Teach us to count our days so that we may acquire a heart of wisdom."

How do we make each day count?

A highly charged executive, we are told, wanted to inspire his employees to be prompt in discharging their duties and completing their assigned tasks. So all around his office and factory, he placed a number of large signs reading: "Do It Now!"

The results, unhappily, were scarcely what he had hoped for. Within two weeks his cashier disappeared with some $10,000; his head bookkeeper left town with his most efficient secretary; every office worker asked for a raise; the factory people called a strike; and the office boy joined the Marines.

Despite the unanticipated consequences of his advice, the executive dispensed some wise counsel that we need to hear and to follow. So many of us postpone the business of living. We're so busy preparing for some future goal that we forget to live in the present.

Dr. William Moulton Marston, a psychologist, asked 3,000 people this brief question: "What do you have to live for?" He was shocked to find that ninety-four percent of his respondents were simply enduring the present while they waited for the future.

They were waiting for "something" to happen—waiting for children to grow up and become independent; waiting to pay off the mortgage; waiting for the day when they could take a long deferred trip; waiting for the leisure that retirement would bring. While they were waiting, life was passing them by, unenjoyed and unappreciated.

Too often, too many of us overlook the poet's simple truth:

"I have no Yesterdays,
   Time took them away;
   Tomorrow may not be,
   But I have today."

Having stated this all-too-obvious truth, we then discover, as our unhappy executive did, that we have not necessarily solved our fundamental human dilemma. The question immediately confronting us is: "How shall we use today?" The way we answer this question determines the very texture of our lives.

In Genesis we read different answers given to this crucial question by Esau and his father Isaac at separate junctures in their lives.

For Esau, that moment came when he was asked to trade his birthright for a bowl of lentil soup. There was surely ample other food available, but Esau wanted only the lentil soup. He wanted what he wanted, when he wanted it. He did not believe in delayed gratification. Why should he? "Behold, I am going to die," he reasoned, "so of what use is my birthright to me?" (Gen. 25:32).

He surely used today—to appease his stomach, to gratify his physical needs. If he had to surrender his birthright in the process, so what? You can't eat a birthright. In his attitude and actions he anticipated Isaiah's hedonistic contemporaries whose self-indulgent motto was: "Let us eat and drink, for tomorrow we die."

Isaac's response to his human fragility and life's unpredictability was quite different. "I am old now," he said to Esau, "and I do not know how soon I may die . . . Go bring me something to eat so that I may bless you before I die" (Gen. 27:24).

Isaac was also going to use today—to be a source of blessing to others.

It may very well be that our tradition dealt quite harshly with Esau precisely because he trivialized life, reducing its awesome grandeur to the gratification of the stomach, dehumanizing it by forgetting that he also had a soul that needed nourishment.

Esau's descendants are legion. We live in an age when the media excite our appetite for instant gratification, instant relief from pain, instant rise to fame. Multimillion-dollar lotteries also stimulate our fantasies about instant riches. Underneath it all, like an uninvited skeleton at the wedding feast, lurks the ominous possibility of the instant destruction of the human race in a nuclear holocaust.

At such a time, the temptation to use today mindlessly and carelessly and selfishly is more than many can resist. And yet resist it we must—for our own salvation and for the preservation of all that makes us worth saving.

Eldad Ran was killed in Israel's War of Independence at the age of 20. Before he died, he left us a legacy containing wisdom that belies the youthfulness of its author. He wrote: "Lately I've been thinking about what the goal of life should be. At best, man's life is short . . . The years of life do not satisfy the hunger for life. What then shall we do during this time?

"We can reach either of two conclusions. The first is that since life is so short, we should enjoy it as much as possible. The second is that precisely because life is short . . . we should dedicate life to a sacred and worthy goal . . . I am slowly coming to the conclusion that life by itself is worth little unless it serves something greater than itself."

Jerusalem Reunited—
Let's Celebrate!

JERUSALEM IS MENTIONED in the Bible 750 times. Zion, another name for Jerusalem, appears 180 times. Different appellations of the city—Mount Moriah, City of David, Temple Mount, Holy City, etc.—appear an additional several hundred times. All in all, there are some 2000 references to Jerusalem in the Hebrew Scriptures.

In Rabbinic writings the number of references is even greater. How the Sages felt about Jerusalem is revealed in this passage:

> "Ten measures of beauty were given to the world, Jerusalem took nine.
> Ten measures of suffering were given to the world, Jerusalem took nine.
> Ten measures of heroism were given to the world, Jerusalem took nine.
> Ten measures of wisdom were given to the world, Jerusalem took nine.
> Ten measures of Torah were given to the world, Jerusalem took nine."
>
> (Avot d'Rabbi Natan 48)

This preoccupation with Jerusalem has long been one of our most magnificent obsessions. About 2500 years ago, our ancestors tasted the bitterness of exile for the first time. As they sat by the rivers of Babylon, they wept when they remembered the glory that once was Zion. Had they been normal, rational people they would have done what other normal, rational people did after they were driven out of their homeland. Other people forgot about it, and they went about the business of getting themselves adjusted to their new surroundings.

Had our ancestors acted similarly, the story of Judaism would have ended there. And like every other people which suffered banishment from its native land, the Jewish people would also have disappeared from the scene of history.

But our ancestors were neither normal nor rational. When their captors asked them to sing one of their Zion songs, they answered, "How can we sing the Lord's song on foreign soil?" Having spurned the invitation to sing or play their harps which they had hung on willow trees, they then went on to make a strange and terrible vow. "If I forget you, O Jerusalem, let my right hand forget its cunning. Let my tongue cleave to the roof of my mouth, if I remember you not; if I set not Jerusalem above my chief joy" (Psalms 137:5-6).

Even stranger than the vow was the fact that our people kept it. We didn't forget Jerusalem. Our daily prayers yearned for the rebuilding of Jerusalem. Our synagogues were oriented toward Jerusalem. Under the canopy the groom broke a glass in remembrance of the shattered Temple which lay in ruins. On Tishah be-Av we fasted and wept over the destruction of Jerusalem. When we painted our homes we left one corner unpainted, because no home was ever complete as long as Jerusalem was unbuilt. We concluded both the Passover *Seder* and Yom Kippur with the prayerful hope: "Next year in Jerusalem." The instinct to remember, the pledge not to forget, were always at work devising new mnemonics to keep Jerusalem always in the forefront of Jewish consciousness, Jewish dreams and Jewish hopes.

We can, therefore, imagine the deep and bitter frustration Jews in Israel felt between 1948 and 1967 when Jordan did not permit any Jews to enter the Old City of Jerusalem or approach the Western Wall. This in spite of the General Armistice Agreement of 1949 which expressly declared that Jordan "will allow free access to the Holy Places and cultural institutions, and use of the cemetery on the Mount of Olives."

Thus we understand the feelings of joy that overwhelmed the Jews in Israel and throughout the world when the electrifying news was broadcast on the third day of the Six Day War that the Old City had been recaptured from Jordan in the war that Jordan initiated.

Over Israeli radio an incredulous people heard the Chief Chaplain of the Israeli Defence Forces sound the Shofar and then speak these words:

> "I am speaking to you from the Western Wall, remnant of our Holy Temple.
> 'Comfort ye, comfort ye My people, says your God!'
> 'This is the day for which we have hoped, let us be glad and rejoice in His Salvation!' "

That day on the Hebrew calendar was the 28th day of Iyyar. That day was to be designated as Yom Yerushalayim, Jerusalem Day, and it was added to the Jewish calendar as a day of rejoicing and thanksgiving.

Let us celebrate!

Our Magnificent Obsession

DURING A SINGLE WEEK one television channel showed "The Ten Commandments," while other channels featured programs that broke six of them.

This melancholy coincidence illustrates the very observation made by an astute observer of the contemporary scene: "There's no need for a period in punctuation anymore. Nobody stops at anything."

However shabbily the Ten Commandments are treated today, their pronouncement on Mount Sinai some 3000 years ago was surely one of the most luminous events in all of human history. The world was never quite the same after that incandescent moment when our ancestors stood at the foot of a quaking mountain and, amidst thunder and lightning, heard the Divine words.

Even Hitler felt the powerful impact of that moment—even if only in a perverse way. Referring to his monstrous creation, Nazism, he called it "the great battle for the liberation from the curse of Mount Sinai." He went on to say: "We are fighting against . . . the curse of the so-called Ten Commandments, against them we are fighting."

Today, on the Festival of Shavuot, we celebrate the "birthday" of the Ten Commandments. Far from being a "curse" from which we need "liberation," the commandments are a blessing to which we need deepened rededication.

Shavuot, "the time of the giving of our Torah," has extraordinary significance for our people. It commemorates the event which burned itself into our soul, molded our character, regulated our behavior and shaped our destiny.

Whatever the impact of Sinai on the course of the subsequent history of mankind in general, one thing is certain. For our people something profoundly revolutionary and irreversible happened there. After Sinai the Jewish people would never be the same.

It was at Sinai that our ancestors heard the heavenly verdict: "On this day you have become a people." A horde of ex-slaves, so recently liberated, was elevated into a consecrated people and given a priceless gift—the Torah. And that made all the difference.

We did not become a people when we threw off the chains of Pharaoh; we became a people when we enlisted in the service of God.

Centuries later the Jewish philosopher Saadiah could write with every justification: "Our people is a people only by virtue of our possession of the Torah."

To possess the Torah meant to be possessed by it. Torah for our people became our magnificent obsession. And thus the Torah grew. Other books were added to the original five, the books that became our Bible, then the Mishnah, the Gemara, Responsa, Commentaries; the works of grammarians, philosophers, mystics, kabbalists, rationalists—all inspired by Torah and included within it.

It was to the study of this entire body of literature that Judaism applied the rabbinic verdict: "The merit of Torah study is equal to all the Commandments."

Torah study was to begin as soon as a child was old enough to read and the process was to continue throughout life. Only death could interrupt it.

We who appeared on the stage of history carrying a Book earned the proud designation—the People of the Book. We carried the Book and the Book carried us. It gave us strength to resist, courage to persevere, and a special dimension of joy in living.

One of the real threats to Jewish survival in America derives from the growing distance between the People of the Book and the books of our people. More and more of our people know less and less about the rich heritage of our people accumulated over long centuries of spiritual and intellectual creativity. Ignorance leads to indifference and indifference leads to loss of identity. An empty sack cannot stand.

The words of Ahad Ha'am are no less true in contemporary America than they were in early twentieth century Russia where they were written: "Learning! Learning! Learning!" That is the secret of Jewish survival.

Long before Ahad Ha'am, our Sages emphasized the crucial centrality of study in two rhetorical questions: "If you have acquired knowledge what do you lack? If you lack knowledge what have you acquired?"

Rabbis Harold Kushner and Jack Riemer, have summoned us to study and acquaint ourselves with our extravagant legacy. Their words are especially meaningful as we approach Shavuot and once again face Mount Sinai:

> "We owe it to our ancestors to keep Torah alive;
> They struggled and suffered to preserve our way of life;
> They knew this to be their most precious gift to us.
>
> We owe it to our children to keep Torah alive;
> For why should they be spiritual paupers
> When the riches of this heritage can be theirs?
>
> We owe it to the world to keep Torah alive;
> This is a message which the world needs to hear.
>
> We owe it to God to continue as a people,
> To share His dream, to bear witness to His sovereignty,
> And to live the words of Torah."

Accepting Life's Coercions

THE LATE Rabbi Stephen S. Wise was once seated at a banquet next to a woman who tried to impress him with her exalted lineage. "One of my ancestors," she said proudly, "witnessed the signing of the Declaration of Independence." The rabbi could not resist replying: "My ancestors were present at the giving of the Ten Commandments."

The Festival of Shavuot marks the traditional anniversary of that historic occasion when our ancestors heard the Divine voice proclaim the words which have probably had a profounder benevolent impact on all of subsequent history than any other recorded words— the Ten Commandments.

The revolutionary moment happened some 3200 years ago in a harsh desert under a broiling sun. There was no radio reporter or television camera to record the event. The audience was a motley horde of ex-slaves who had so very recently escaped from centuries of oppression. But that fateful encounter forged them into a people, a people whose primary task it would be to treasure those words, preserve them and live by them.

That they honored faithfully their commitment in the face of the most incredible odds is attested to by the fact that we are here, a vital creative Jewish people preparing once again to observe Shavuot, "The time of the giving of our Torah."

Our Sages speculated on the circumstances under which our

ancestors accepted the Torah. According to one tradition the Almighty offered the Torah to one nation after another who each rejected it because of some prohibition it contained which they found objectionable. When He offered it to our ancestors they eagerly accepted the Torah without even bothering to inquire about its contents.

Another tradition gives a radically different version. It claims that the Almighty inverted Mount Sinai like a bowl over the heads of our ancestors and said to them: "If you accept My Torah well and good; if not this shall be your burial place."

Is it possible to reconcile these two conflicting traditions? Can we give credence to the tradition that our ancestors accepted the Torah willingly, while at the same time believing that they accepted the Torah under ultimate coercion?

Perhaps on deeper reflection the two traditions are indeed compatible. Perhaps they point to a wise strategy for facing life—we must learn to accept what we cannot change, we must translate our coercions into affirmations.

Life is full of coercions. Indeed, life itself is a coercion. As an ancient rabbi long ago told us: "Against your will were you born." And the young never tire of reminding their parents: "I didn't ask to be born." One of Sholom Aleichem's characters makes the wry observation: "The way life is, you're better off not to be born. But who can be so lucky? Maybe one in ten thousand."

The Talmud records a philosophical debate between the schools of Shammai and Hillel on this very question. "Was it better for man to have been created than not to have been created." The discussion continued without resolution for two-and-a-half years. Finally they put the question to a vote and it was decided that it were better for man not to have been created. "However," they added, "having been created let him pay heed to his actions."

Life is indeed a matter of coercion but we must accept it gladly and use it wisely. George Santayana reflected the spirit of our Sages when he wrote: "That life is worth living is the most necessary of assumptions, and were it not assumed, the most impossible of conclusions."

On Shavuot we also recite Yizkor, a reminder of another powerful coercion, death. The Sage who reminded us that we were born against our will didn't fail to add "against your will you will die."

Death is cruel. It robs us of our loved ones and ultimately inflicts the crushing assault on human personality—obliteration.

And yet here, too, our Sages taught us to accept this bitter coercion. They gave a remarkable interpretation to the Biblical verse: "And God saw all that He had made and, behold, it was very good." "Very good," they said, refers to death.

What a tremendous affirmation! They weren't thumbing their noses at death but they understood that death plays a vital role in life. We cherish life precisely because we are aware of its transience. The urge to create, the passion to perfect, the sheer joy of welcoming each day—all the noblest of human enterprises and emotions flourish in the soil of human mortality. They would vanish if life on earth were an endless unrelieved process.

Lastly, let us consider that being a Jew is also a matter of coercion. Except for the welcome converts in our midst the rest of us did not choose to be born Jewish. We were born that way. How shall we deal with this coercion?

We can lament this fact, be ashamed of it, try to suppress or deny it. Or we can accept it with pride, gratitude and joy in the spirit of the prayer we recite each morning:

"How fortunate we are!
How good is our portion!
How pleasant our lot!
How beautiful our heritage!"

Fate is what we are given. Destiny is what we make of what is given to us. We cannot choose our fate but we can shape our destiny. And in that choice lies all the difference.

On Being Unreasonable

SOME YEARS AGO there appeared an anthology entitled, *I Believe*. It contained the personal creeds and convictions of some of the most prominent people of the world. One of these was the renowned American novelist Pearl Buck. In setting forth her philosophy she said that "The primary attitude toward life must be acceptance," and that this acceptance of life is the most significant act of the human mind.

Acceptance is, indeed, one of the crucial qualities for grown-up living. We have to be able to accept economic losses. Most of us can remember the disastrous financial crash of 1929. The disaster was not, primarily, that people lost fortunes, but that many could not accept these losses and go on.

We desperately need the power of acceptance when we, or those we love, sustain a loss of health or become handicapped. We live in a tension-filled society where it is not uncommon for a man in his prime to become physically handicapped by an ailment. At such a time he has to be able to resign himself to more limited activity, a more deliberate pace of living and to go on with a handicap.

We need the power of acceptance most urgently when we sustain the loss of a loved one. How tempting and how human it is to be filled with despair over our possibilities of ever leading a meaningful existence again. Or we can become overwhelmed by self-pity, which has accurately been labeled as "a passport to insanity."

Important as it undeniably is to be able to accept things as they are, there are times when it is no less important to refuse to accept things as they are, when we must reject things as they are, refuse to resign ourselves to the existing situation.

A massive illustration of this truth is provided by Tishah be-Av, the Ninth of Av, which is observed as a day of fasting and mourning.

Tishah be-Av commemorates the destruction of the first and second Temples in Jerusalem. By coincidence, both disasters, separated by 656 years, fell on the Ninth of Av.

The observance of this grim anniversary for almost 2,000 years served as a dramatic refusal to accept exile and the loss of sovereignty. Other peoples who were driven out of their homeland shrugged their shoulders in despair, and proceeded to accept their new circumstances. The Jew alone refused to accept the new situation as permanent.

Every Tishah be-Av was a passionate protest against existing conditions. And if in our day the Jewish people succeeded in regaining their independence, much of the credit must go to their stubborn, persistent refusal to accept things as they were.

This is true of every noteworthy achievement. Trace any human advance or discovery or invention far enough and you will find its origin in the heart of a person who refused to accept things as they were.

George Bernard Shaw conveyed this thought with characteristic wit: "The reasonable man," he said, "adapts himself to the world. The unreasonable one persists in trying to adapt the world to himself. Therefore, all progress depends on the unreasonable man."

In this sense, it is of vital importance that we become unreasonable.

In our time there is so much that cries for improvement in the world around us, and so much that needs mending within each of us, that we simply cannot afford to accept things as they are.

Perhaps our theme can best be summed up in the familiar prayer: "Grant me, O God, the serenity to accept the things I cannot change, the courage to change the things I can change, and the wisdom to know one from the other."

Living Up to Our Masks

DURING THE eighteenth and nineteenth centuries, a favorite form of social entertainment for European aristocrats was the masqued ball. The guests would each come in costume and wear some disguise. When the midnight hour struck, off came the masks and each guest stood revealed in his or her true identity. A Swedish theologian was thinking of these masqued balls when he said something which applies not only to the aristocracy. "There comes a midnight hour when all men must unmask."

For us Jews, this night of *Selihot* is such a midnight hour. Tonight we usher in the season when we are summoned to appear before God without masks or disguises. We stand stripped of all pretense before Him who, in the words of our Bible, "does not look as man looks; for man looks with the eyes but God looks into the heart." He is the "searcher of hearts" and the "revealer of all hidden things." Masks are not much help.

The habit of wearing masks is one which all of us have cultivated. The very word "person" in English comes from the Latin "personna" which means "a mask." In the theatre of ancient Rome each character wore a distinctive mask and his identity was reflected in his "personna." To be a person is to wear a mask.

Gilbert and Sullivan put the matter in poetic form:

> "Things are seldom what they seem,
> Skimmed milk masquerades as cream."

Masks, it would seem, are instruments of deception and whether we delude ourselves or others is immaterial. To attempt to live our lives behind masks is as treacherous as erecting a skyscraper on a foundation of sand. John Erskine gave eminently sound advice when he urged, "Put on what man you are; put off the mask."

And yet, after we have said all this there is a lingering feeling that we have not explored this truth completely. The fact is that certain masks are quite indispensable for living. Were we entirely incapable of masking our true feelings, we often could not perform our assigned tasks.

The salesman soliciting an order may be quite worried about his sick little boy at home, but unless he can put on the mask of enthusiasm over his product, he will not be able to provide for his sick child. The restaurant hostess may be heartsick over a shattered marriage, but unless she can wear the mask of radiant good cheer she may soon find herself without a job. The professional counselor may have a host of personal problems gnawing away at him, but unless he can put on the mask of certainty and composure he will soon lose his usefulness to those who seek his aid. The grieving widow may feel an awesome burden of sorrow oppressing her heart but if she cannot manage to mask her true feelings, she may find friends hard to come by. And any one of us may find ourselves at the bedside of a dear friend or a loved one suffering from a fatal disease, and unless we can put on the mask of hopefulness and confidence we will betray our mission of mercy. All of us, at one time or another, must play Pagliacci wearing the mask of the carefree, laughing clown over a face distorted by pain and twisted in agony. As a temporary facade behind which to conceal untimely emotions, masks are not only permissible, they are priceless.

Moreover, we could all grow into finer human beings if we learned to wear the mask of the finest human being we know—not in order to pretend to be what we are not, but rather as a means of aspiring to be what we can become. If we would become kinder and more sympathetic, we would do well to assume the pose and strike the attitude of the kindly and sympathetic person. If we would become more understanding and more merciful, we could profitably don the masks of understanding and mercy. Someone has said with fine insight, "Act human and you will become human." In the very process of playing the role of a better person, we can take an impressive forward stride in actually becoming better. All aspiration is partial realization.

One of the most dramatic illustrations of this truth was provided by the actor Richard Berry Harrison, who played the role of "De Lawd" in the original production of "Green Pastures." Harrison was chosen for the role because of his powerful build and deep resonant voice, not necessarily for any spiritual qualities. People who watched him perform in the play testified, as did Harrison himself, that after 1700 performances as the Lord, he had become a highly spiritualized individual. As he himself explained it, he strove to become godlike, to be worthy of the role he played. He tried with conspicuous success to live up to his mask. He demonstrated the truth of Professor Hocking's assertion: "There is a deep tendency in human nature to become like that which we imagine ourselves to be."

Let us select our masks carefully, and then let us live up to our masks.